Wonder-Under®
Scrap Happy
Christmas

Oxmoor House®

Wonder-Under® Scrap Happy Christmas
from the *Fun with Fabric* series

©1999 by Oxmoor House, Inc.
Book Division of Southern Progress Corporation
P.O. Box 2463, Birmingham, Alabama 35201

Published by Oxmoor House, Inc., and
Leisure Arts, Inc.

Library of Congress Catalog Number: 98-68201
Hardcover ISBN: 0-8487-1874-7
Softcover ISBN: 0-8487-1875-5
Manufactured in the United States of America
First Printing 1999

Editor-in-Chief: Nancy Fitzpatrick Wyatt
Senior Crafts Editor: Susan Ramey Cleveland
Senior Editor, Copy and Homes:
    Olivia Kindig Wells
Art Director: James Boone

Wonder-Under® Scrap Happy Christmas
Contributing Editor: Cecile Y. Nierodzinski
Copy Editor: L. Amanda Owens
Editorial Assistant: Heather Averett
Associate Art Director: Cynthia R. Cooper
Designer: Clare Minges
Illustrator: Kelly Davis
Senior Photographer: John O'Hagan
Photo Stylist: Linda Baltzell Wright
Senior Production Designer: Larry Hunter
Publishing Systems Administrator: Rick Tucker
Director, Production and Distribution: Phillip Lee
Associate Production Manager:
    Theresa L. Beste
Production Assistant: Faye Porter Bonner

We're Here for You!
We at Oxmoor House are dedicated to serving you with reliable information that expands your imagination and enriches your life. We welcome your comments and suggestions. Please write us at:

Oxmoor House, Inc.
Editor, **Wonder-Under® Scrap Happy Christmas**
2100 Lakeshore Drive
Birmingham, AL 35209

To order additional publications, call 1-205-877-6560.

Pellon and Wonder-Under are registered trademarks of Freudenberg Nonwovens. To locate a Pellon® Wonder-Under® retailer in your area, call 1-800-223-5275.

Contents

Introduction

Jolly Trimmings

Ba Ba Plaid Sheep, page 22

Fanciful Gifts

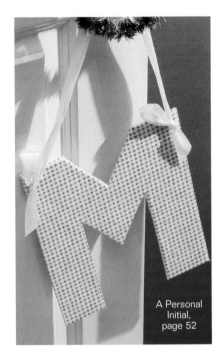

A Personal Initial, page 52

String-of-Lights Nightshirt, page 106

Seasonal Fashions

Table Favors

Tabletop Lanterns, page 124

Introduction

The Christmas season is here once again. Schedules are tighter, time is more precious then ever, and your list of gifts and holiday preparations is getting longer everyday. We know the struggle well. That's why Oxmoor House, Inc., and Freudenberg Nonwovens has teamed up to help you out. Take a deep breath, settle back, and look at what Pellon® Wonder-Under® has in store for you.

Conveniently divided into four chapters, *Wonder-Under® Scrap Happy Christmas* is your solution for easing the hustle and bustle of your Christmas preparations. You'll be able to use your leftover crafting fabrics, papers, and ribbons to make fabulous projects.

Jolly Trimmings is chock-full of home decorating ideas. From wall accents to the classic stocking and tree skirt, there's something for everyone.

Fanciful Gifts gets kids involved in the holiday spirit. Making projects from paper and fabric scraps teamed with Wonder-Under is a real bonus,

limiting the use of messy glue.

Seasonal Fashions combines ready-made garments and specially designed appliqués to boost any holiday wardrobe.

Dress up your table for Christmas dinner, too. **Table Favors** attends to the details of your table, from how-tos on covering your dining chairs to making candy holders for your guests.

The versatility of *Wonder-Under Scrap® Happy Christmas* is that you can use all of the patterns included in this book for your own project ideas. Then try mixing and matching our suggestions with projects from other chapters. And remember, you can always make that Photo Box (page 48) or Crazy Quilt Jewelry (page 46) for yourself.

Wonder-Under is a true time-saver, with no waiting around for it to set and to dry, as with glue. Minutes are saved, getting you that much closer to finishing your holiday list on time. So, enjoy yourself, indulge your creativity, and have a happy holiday.

Jolly Trimmings is your guide to creative home decorating for the holidays. Discover this Snowman Tree Skirt (page 12) and other traditional holiday projects in the pages of this chapter.

Finding it difficult to choose that special present? Look through **Fanciful Gifts** and find something for everyone on your list. Homebaked goodies served in this Breakfast Tray (page 44) will hit the spot on Christmas morning.

Seasonal Fashions offers an array of embel-lished gifts. This denim shirt features a versatile snowflake appliqué. Turn to Let It Snow (page 104) to find out more.

Holiday decorating is not over until your table is complete. Check out **Table Favors** for quick ways to spruce up your usual dinning room setting. Tabletop Lanterns (page 124) set Christmas aglow.

General Instructions

In addition to reading the manufacturer's instructions, take a look
at our informative tips and steps for crafting with Pellon® Wonder-Under®,
as well as how to use the patterns in this book.

Choosing the Correct Weight

Wonder-Under—Regular Weight and Heavy Duty—is available at fabric and crafts stores, off the bolt or in several prepackaged widths and lengths. It also comes in ¾"-wide precut tape, 10 yards long, that is ideal for fusing hems and ribbons.

- Test different weights to find which Wonder-Under best suits the project. Generally, use regular-weight web for lightweight to medium-weight fabrics. For heavyweight fabrics, a heavy-duty web is best. (Heavy Duty Wonder-Under has more glue and, therefore, more "stick.")

- Avoid buying heavy-duty web for an appliquéd garment, as it may add too much stiffness. Use regular-weight web and finish the edges of the appliqué as necessary to ensure a washable garment. (See washable fabric paint under Embellishment Techniques on page 8.)

- Remember that Regular Weight Wonder-Under is usually recommended for projects in this book unless Heavy Duty is specified.

- Read the Wonder-Under package label for tips on its application and washability.

- Try out Wonder-Under on scraps of fabric before you start your actual project. Let the sample cool and then check to see that the fabric pieces have bonded and that the fused layers won't separate.

Perfect Patterns

Wonder-Under is translucent, so you can place the web (paper side up) directly onto a pattern for tracing.

- If a pattern isn't the size you want or need, enlarge or reduce it, using a photocopier.

- If a pattern has an asymmetrical or one-way design, the finished appliqué will be a mirror image of the pattern. So if a pattern points left, the appliqué will point right. In this book, patterns are reversed as necessary.

Fusing Basics

1. If your project has an appliqué pattern, trace the pattern onto the paper (smooth) side of the Wonder-Under. Leaving a margin, cut around the shape.

2. For all Wonder-Under projects, place the web side of the Wonder-Under onto the wrong side of the fabric. Press for 5 seconds with a hot, dry iron. Let the fabric cool. (If some of the Wonder-Under sticks to your iron, remove it with a hot-iron cleaner, available in most notions departments of fabric and crafts stores.) For each appliqué, cut out the shape along the pattern lines.

3. For each appliqué, remove the paper backing from the Wonder-Under.

4. Position the fabric, web side down, on your project. (Fusible items can be held temporarily in place by "touch basting." Touch the item to be fused with the tip of the iron only. If the item is not in the desired position, it can be lifted and repositioned.)

5. To fuse, cover the fabric with a damp pressing cloth, unless otherwise specified. Using an iron heated to the wool setting, press firmly for 10 seconds. (Heavy fabrics may require more time.) Repeat, lifting and pressing until all the fabric is fused.

6. Remove the pressing cloth and iron the fabric to eliminate any excess moisture.

Embellishment Techniques

There is a right finish for every project. Here are some
examples of the varieties of finishes to choose from.

Use washable fabric paints for a terrific no-sew finish. Available at crafts stores, these paints come in
squeezable tubes that allow you to outline an
appliqué with a thin line of paint. Place cardboard
under the appliqué to prevent seepage and follow
the manufacturer's directions for drying time (some
paints require several days to set). Most manufac-
turers recommend washing the finished project in
warm water.

If you prefer a machine-stitched finish, try a decorative zigzag to add security to appliqué edges. Closely
spaced zigzag stitches—or satin stitches—give shapes
strong definition and completely encase raw edges.
Even multiple layers of fabric fused with Heavy Duty
Wonder-Under can be satin-stitched.

Glue twine, rickrack, braid, lace, or other trims to your project to give extra dimension or color.

Add dimension and sparkle with buttons and beads. Sewn or glued in place, these embellishments can represent ornaments, candy, and other objects.

Try fine-tipped fabric markers for easy detail, such as drawing "quilting lines" around the edges of an appliqué. This technique is sometimes called pen stitching.

Jolly
Trimmings

Aroma
Garland,
page 20

Snowman Tree Skirt

Short on time? Then start with a purchased tree skirt
and have your tree dressed in no time at all.

Place on fold.

Materials

Tracing paper

Rotary cutter with straight and wavy
blades

1 yard 72"-wide red felt

Red thread

Pellon® Wonder-Under®

Assorted fabric scraps for
appliqués: white, green, and red
prints; green and red plaids

Cream pearl cotton

Assorted buttons: 18 (⅝"), 6 (½")

Fine-tip permanent black fabric
marker

Instructions

1. Using patterns, trace tree skirt
triangle. Cut out triangle for pattern. With straight blade in rotary
cutter and using joined pattern, cut
6 triangles from red felt.

2. With right sides together and
edges aligned, machine-stitch long
triangle edges with red thread. Do
not sew last triangles together but
leave open for fitting around tree.

3. With wavy blade in rotary cutter,
trim inner circle, unstitched edges,
and outer circle of tree skirt.

4. Using patterns on page 14,
trace 3 hats, 3 brims, 3 bows (pieces
6 and 7), 3 scarves (pieces 3–5),
3 reversed scarves, 3 noses,
3 reversed noses, 3 bodies,
3 reversed bodies, 6 arms, and
6 reversed arms onto paper side of
Wonder-Under. Leaving approximate ½" margin, cut around
Wonder-Under shapes. Press shapes
onto wrong side of fabric scraps.
Cut out shapes along pattern lines.
Remove paper backing. Referring to
photo, center and fuse shapes 1–8,
in that order, on each triangle.

5. Handstitch long strands, using
pearl cotton; tie knots and cut ends
to create scarf trim (see photo). Tie
and knot 3 (⅝") buttons down center front of each snow person, using
pearl cotton. Repeat to attach
1 (½") button to top of each hat
and in center of each bow.

6. Using fabric marker, embellish
appliqués with drawn stitches.

Tree Skirt

Place on fold.

Tree Skirt

Overlap shaded areas of
triangle to continue pattern.

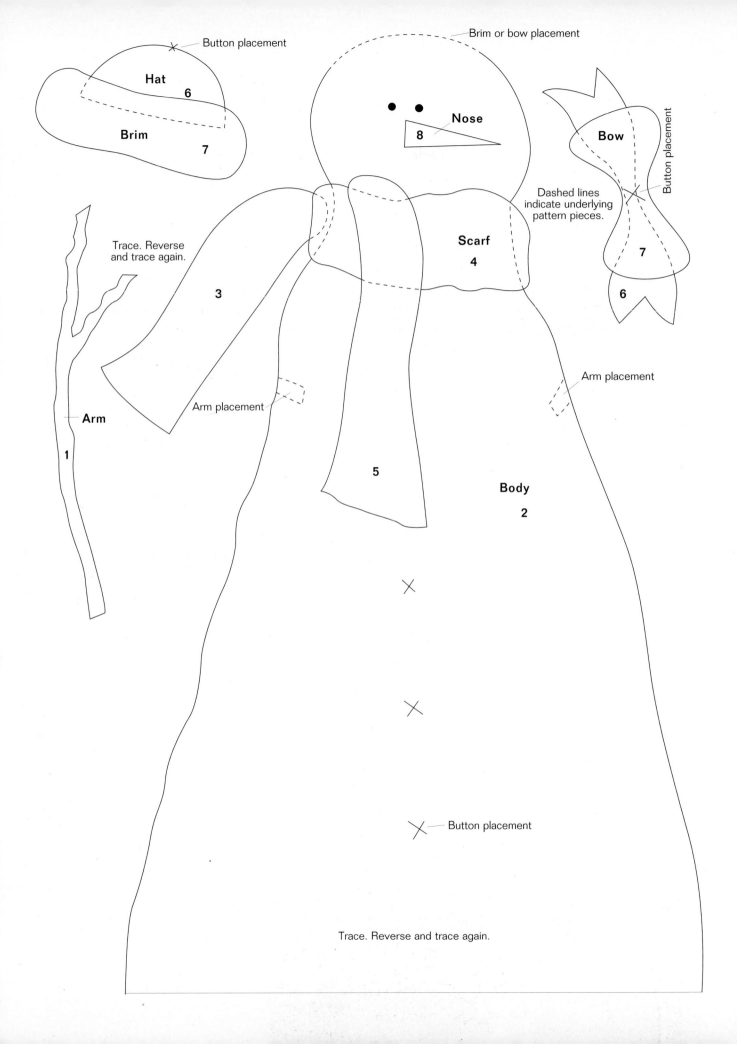

Button placement

Hat

6

Brim

7

Brim or bow placement

Nose

8

Bow

Button placement

Dashed lines
indicate underlying
pattern pieces.

Scarf

4

7

6

Trace. Reverse
and trace again.

3

Arm

1

Arm placement

Arm placement

5

Body

2

Button placement

Trace. Reverse and trace again.

Tree-of-Plenty Banner

This banner is made from a table runner, cut in half.
So make one to give and another to keep.

Materials

Purchased plain table runner with
   tassel
Assorted fabric scraps for
   appliqués: red plaid, Christmas
   prints, green print
¾"-wide Pellon® Wonder-Under®
   fusible tape
½ yard 1"-wide green grosgrain
   ribbon
Pellon® Wonder-Under®
1 skein green embroidery floss
Buttons: 3 (¾") green, 2 (½") red
Red thread
Jewelry glue
3 (5-mm) half-round black beads

Instructions

1. Wash, dry, and iron table runner
and fabrics. Do not use fabric softener in washer or dryer.

2. Measure and mark 33" from
1 point of table runner. Cut across
runner at mark. Press fusible tape
onto wrong side of cut edge of runner. Remove paper backing. Turn
under and fuse raw edge in place.

3. Cut ribbon into 3 (6") pieces.
Cut and press 1" of fusible tape
onto each end of each ribbon.
Remove paper backing. Fuse ends of
each ribbon length together to form
loop. In same manner, fuse ribbon
loops to wrong side of banner top
(see photo).

4. Using patterns below and on page 17 , trace 4 tree trunks, 1 star, 1 gingerbread man, 1 candy cane, 1 tree, 1 stocking, 1 dove, 1 mitten, 1 heart, 1 pot, and 1 each of bottom, middle, and top branches onto paper side of Wonder-Under. Leaving approximate ½" margin, cut around Wonder-Under shapes. Press shapes onto wrong side of fabric scraps. Cut out shapes along pattern lines. Remove paper backing. Referring to photos, arrange and fuse shapes on banner front.

5. Using 3 strands of embroidery floss, blanket-stitch around all appliqué edges.

Using matching floss or thread, stitch 1 green button to front of each hanging loop and 2 red buttons to gingerbread man. Using jewelry glue, glue 2 beads on gingerbread man and 1 bead on dove for eyes (see photo).

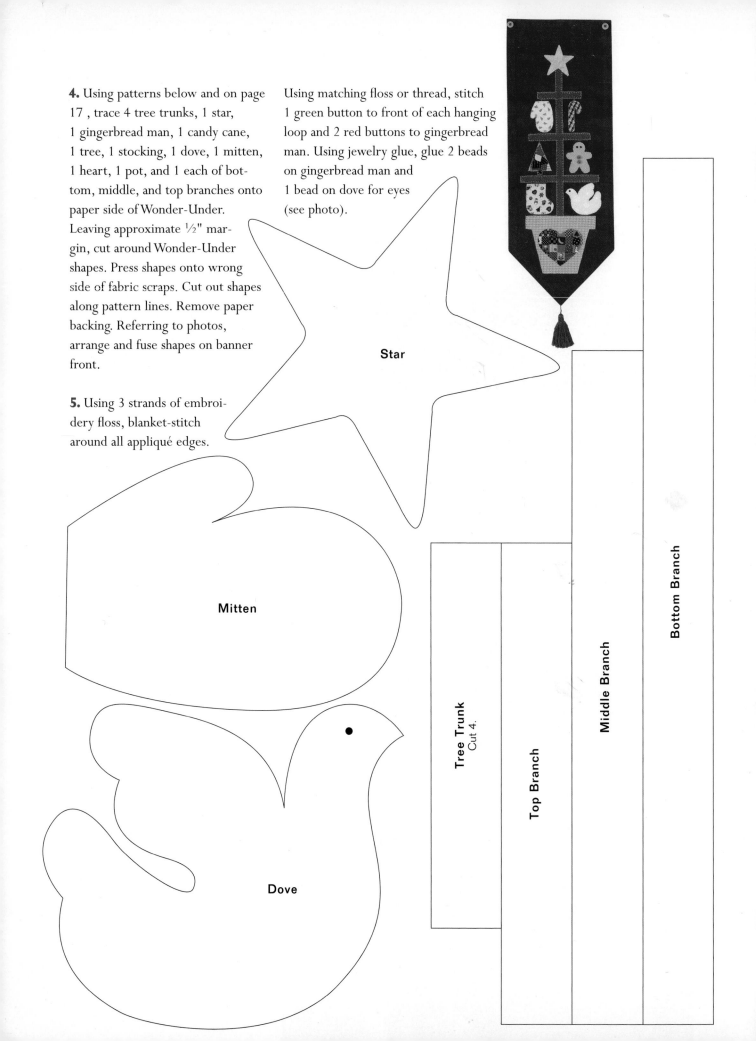

Star

Mitten

Dove

Tree Trunk
Cut 4.

Top Branch

Middle Branch

Bottom Branch

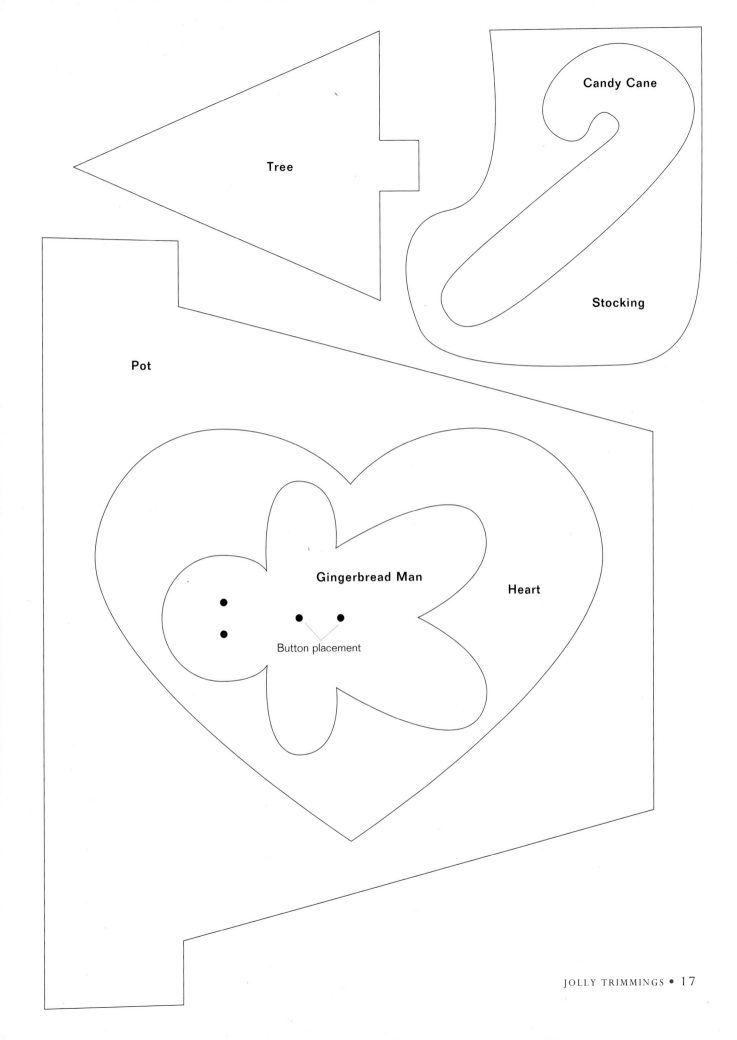

Tree

Candy Cane

Stocking

Pot

Gingerbread Man

Heart

Button placement

Homespun Throw

Bring the warmth of winter's warmest outdoor accessories indoors with these mitten and hat motifs on a cozy throw.

Materials

Purchased plain throw
Assorted fabric scraps for
    appliqués: Christmas plaids,
    red, green
Pellon® Wonder-Under®
14 (¾" to 1") assorted buttons
Coordinating thread
Red pearl cotton

Instructions

NOTE: If throw will be washed frequently, outline motifs with coordinating dimensional fabric paint or blanket-stitch around appliqués.

1. Wash, dry, and iron throw and fabrics. Do not use fabric softener in washer or dryer.

2. Using patterns, trace 7 mittens, 7 reversed mittens, 14 cuffs, 7 hats, and 7 brims onto paper side of Wonder-Under. Leaving approximate ½" margin, cut around Wonder-Under shapes. Press shapes onto wrong side of fabric scraps.

Cut out shapes along pattern lines. Remove paper backing. Referring to photo, fuse shapes onto throw.

3. For each hat, cut coordinating fabric scrap into 2" x 3" rectangle. Gather rectangle at center and secure with thread. Cut ¼" toward middle of rectangle on each short side to make pom-pom. Handstitch pom-pom to hat center through all thicknesses.

4. Thread pearl cotton through 1 button at corner of each mitten cuff. Tie and knot each button to secure.

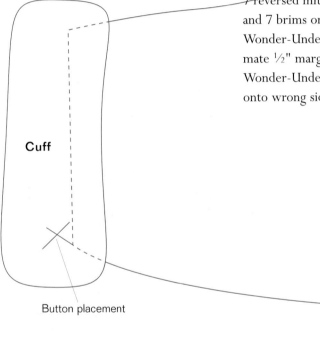

Cuff

Button placement

Mitten
Trace. Reverse and trace again.

Pom-pom placement

Dashed lines
indicate underlying
pattern pieces.

Hat

Brim

Aroma Garland

Add cinnamon essential oil to each stuffed heart
to enhance this decoration's spicy scent.

Materials (Makes 72"-long garland.)

Tracing paper
¼ yard cream fabric
Cream thread
Pellon® Wonder-Under®
Assorted fabric scraps for appliqués: green print, gold print, Christmas prints
Fine-tip permanent black fabric marker
Polyester stuffing
Dollmaker's hand needle
1 skein cream embroidery floss
8 (2½"-long) cinnamon sticks
2 (¾"-diameter) plastic rings
Jewelry glue
27 (¼" to 1") assorted red and green buttons

Instructions

1. Wash, dry, and iron fabrics. Do not use fabric softener in washer or dryer.

2. Using pattern, trace and cut out heart. Cut 18 hearts from cream fabric. Group hearts into 9 pairs. With right sides together and raw edges aligned, machine-stitch around each heart pair, using ¼" seam allowance and leaving small opening for turning and stuffing. Turn each heart right side out and press.

3. Using patterns, trace 5 trees, 4 large stars, and 5 small stars onto paper side of Wonder-Under. Leaving approximate ½" margin, cut around Wonder-Under shapes. Press shapes onto wrong side of fabric scraps. Cut out shapes along pattern lines. Remove paper backing.

Referring to photo, center and fuse shapes on hearts.

4. Using fabric marker, embellish appliqués with pen stitching.

5. Stuff hearts with polyester stuffing. Using hand needle and thread, slipstitch opening closed.

6. Using hand needle and 6 strands of embroidery floss knotted at 1 end, thread needle through upper portion of 1 tree heart (see photo). String 1 cinnamon stick through needle and then add 1 star heart. Continue alternating cinnamon sticks and hearts until finished. Knot ends of embroidery floss.

7. Whipstitch 1 plastic ring to each end heart for hanger.

8. Using glue, embellish appliqués with assorted buttons. Let dry.

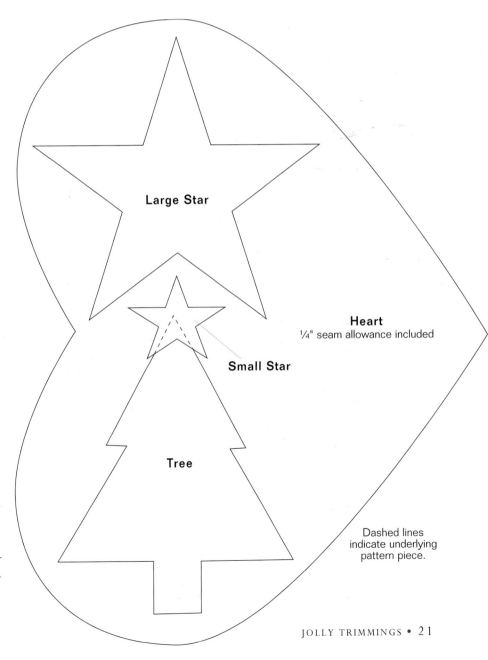

Large Star

Small Star

Tree

Heart
¼" seam allowance included

Dashed lines indicate underlying pattern piece.

Ba Ba Plaid Sheep

Change the holly leaves to oak or maple to make this a year-round wall hanging.

Materials

Fabrics: 1⅓ yards red print; ½ yard green print; white-and-black plaid, black, and green scraps for appliqués

Pellon® Wonder-Under®

Threads: black, light green, dark green, red

Red beads: 48 (5-mm), 24 (2-mm)

¾ yard craft batting

2 (¾"-diameter) plastic rings

Instructions

NOTE: If wall hanging will be washed frequently, outline motifs with coordinating dimensional fabric paint.

1. Wash, dry, and iron fabrics. Do not use fabric softener in washer or dryer.

2. Cut red fabric into 2 (24") squares. Fold 1 square in half and then in half again. Press along fold lines to divide square; unfold square and lay flat. Set aside remaining square.

3. Using patterns below and on page 24, trace 1 body, 1 reversed body, 1 head, 1 reversed head, 1 ear, 1 reversed ear, 1 tail, 1 reversed tail, 2 rings, 18 small holly leaves, and 48 large holly leaves onto paper side of Wonder-Under. Leaving approximate ½" margin, cut around Wonder-Under shapes. Press shapes onto wrong side of fabric scraps. Cut out shapes along pattern lines. Remove paper backing. Referring to photo, fuse shapes onto divided red fabric square.

4. With black thread, edgestitch close to inside edges of each appliqué. Alternating light and dark green thread, edgestitch holly leaves and rings. Using red thread, sew 3 (5-mm) beads to middle of each large holly-leaf cluster. For each small holly-leaf cluster, use 3 (2-mm) beads.

5. Cut craft batting into 1 (24") square. Stack 1 red square (wrong side up), batting, and appliquéd square (right side up), aligning raw edges. Using red thread, machine-stitch along pressed fold lines through all thicknesses (see photo).

6. To make binding, cut 1 (15⅝") square from green fabric. Cut square in half diagonally. Referring to Diagram 1, with right sides facing, machine-stitch triangles together ¼" from edge. Press seam open. Mark 2½"-wide strips on joined piece (Diagram 2). With right sides facing, extend corner points 2½" past natural matching points (Diagram 3). Stitch together ¼" from edge. Cut binding strip, starting with 1 extended point and following marked strips. With wrong sides facing, press binding in half lengthwise.

7. With right sides facing and raw edges aligned, pin edge of binding to appliquéd side of wall hanging. Stitch binding ¼" from edge through all thicknesses. Overlap ends and handstitch together. Turn binding to back of wall hanging, folding under raw edges. Whipstitch binding in place.

8. Handstitch 1 plastic ring to back of wall hanging at top of each corner for hanger.

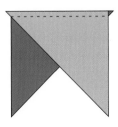

Diagram 1

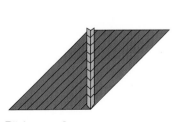

Diagram 2

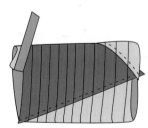

Diagram 3

Ring

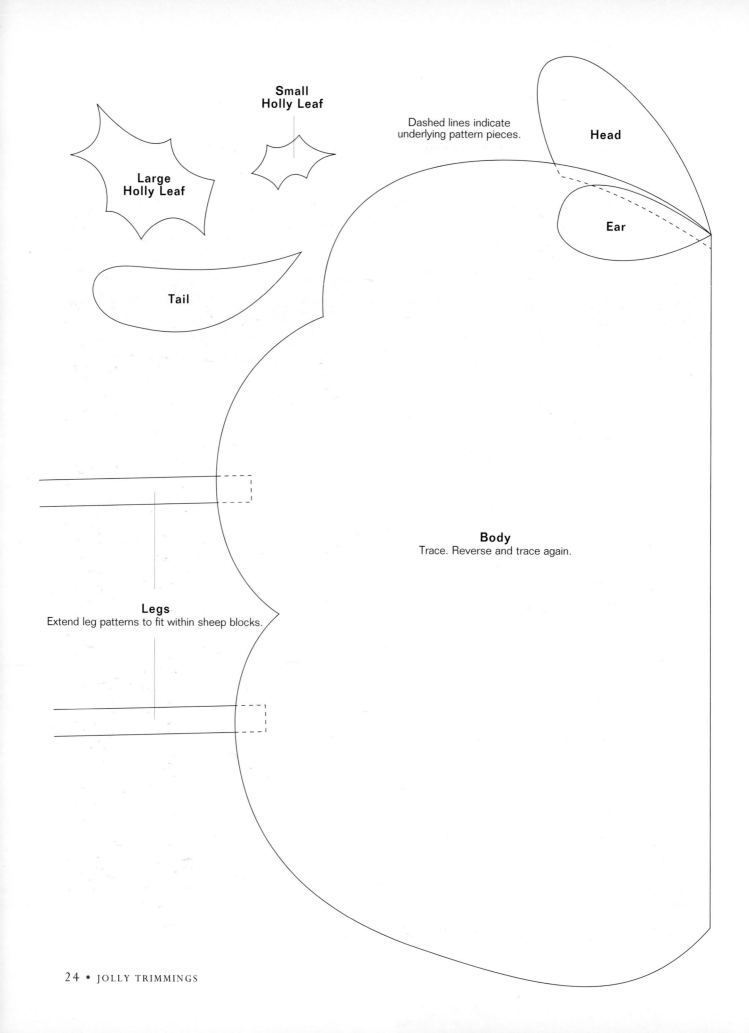

Small Holly Leaf

Large Holly Leaf

Dashed lines indicate underlying pattern pieces.

Head

Ear

Tail

Body
Trace. Reverse and trace again.

Legs
Extend leg patterns to fit within sheep blocks.

Festive Mailbox Cover

This jolly painted canvas cover won't melt even if your holiday skies are sunny.

Materials

Fabrics: 18" x 40" piece each white canvas and white fabric; black, orange, brown, and blue polka-dot scraps for appliqués
Pinking shears
Craft paints: white, green, black
Paintbrush
Pellon® Heavy Duty Wonder-Under®
Hot-glue gun and glue sticks
Black buttons: 2 (1"), 3 (2")
1½ yards 1"-wide grosgrain ribbon

Instructions

1. Cut raw edges of canvas with pinking shears. Using white paint and paintbrush, paint 1 side of canvas. Let dry. With green paint and using loose brushstrokes, paint diagonal lines across canvas (see photo). Let dry. Fold canvas in half widthwise, with painted side out.

2. Draw 2 (20"-tall) snowman shapes onto paper side of Wonder-Under. Leaving approximate ½" margin, cut around Wonder-Under shapes. Press shapes onto wrong side of white fabric. Cut out shapes along pattern lines. Remove paper backing. Referring to photo, center and fuse 1 shape each on front and back of folded canvas.

3. Using patterns below and on page 27, trace 1 scarf, 1 reversed scarf, 1 nose, 1 reversed nose, 1 short arm, 1 reversed short arm, 1 long arm, 1 reversed long arm, 1 hat, and 1 reversed hat onto paper side of Wonder-Under. Leaving approximate ½" margin, cut around Wonder-Under shapes. Press shapes onto wrong side of fabric scraps. Cut out shapes along pattern lines. Remove paper backing. Referring to photo, fuse appliqués 1–4, in that order, onto 1 snowman. Repeat to fuse

reversed appliqués 1–4 onto remaining snowman. To make fringe on each snowman scarf, make short vertical cuts into unfused ends of scarf.

4. For each snowman, using black craft paint and handle end of paintbrush, make 7 black dots to form mouth (see photo). Let dry. Using hot-glue gun and glue sticks, glue 1" buttons in place for eyes and 2" buttons evenly spaced down front of snowman.

5. To attach cover to mailbox, fold ribbon in half to find center. On wrong side of cover, place ribbon center on top of cover center. Hot-glue 10" of ribbon along middle of cover, with 5" on each side of cover center.

6. Tie cover to mailbox, centering cover and tying ribbon ends in bow underneath box.

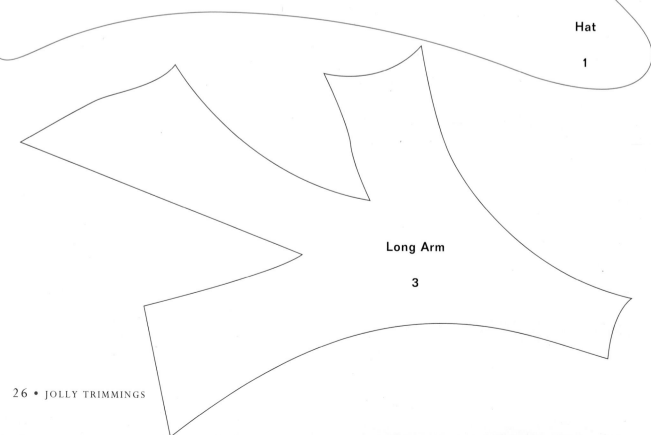

Hat

1

Long Arm

3

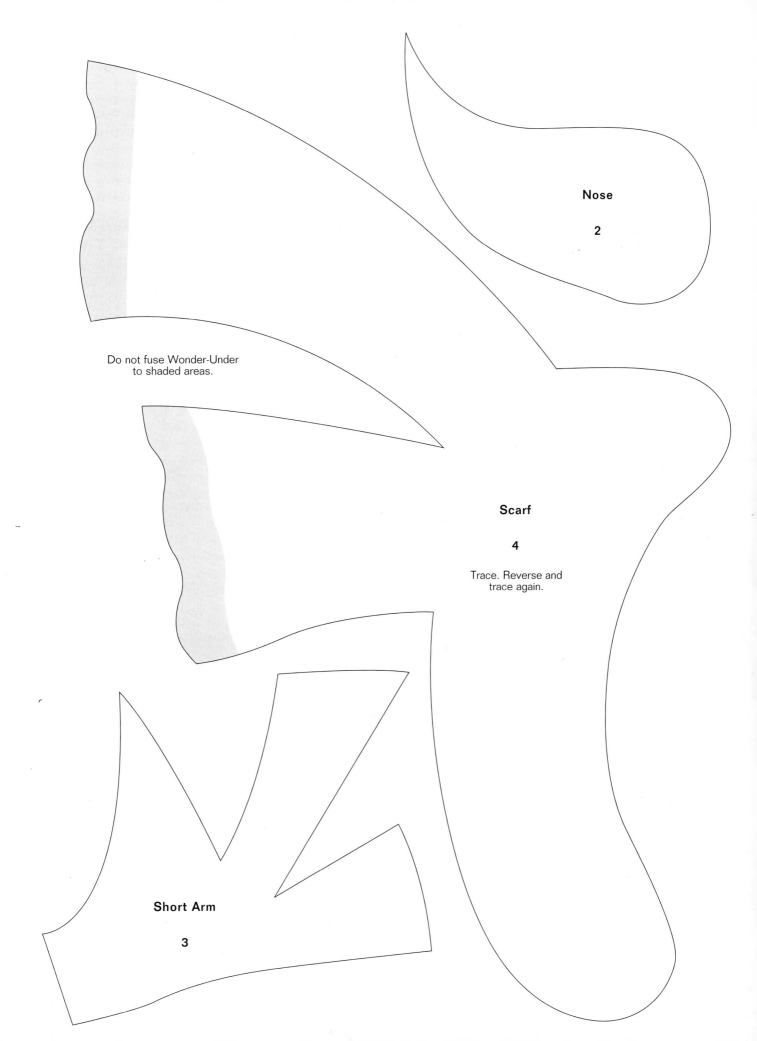

Do not fuse Wonder-Under
to shaded areas.

Nose

2

Scarf

4

Trace. Reverse and
trace again.

Short Arm

3

Indoor Wreath

Instead of using perishable greenery, substitute this fabric wreath
that will last for many Christmases to come.

Materials

Fabrics: 2 yards cream print;
   ¼ yard each red print, gold print,
   green print, and Christmas print
Thread: cream, red
12"-diameter Styrofoam wreath
Pellon® Wonder-Under®
Small saw or serrated knife
Low temperature hot-glue gun and
   glue sticks
Safety pin (optional)
1 (¾"-diameter) plastic ring

Instructions

1. Wash, dry, and iron fabrics. Do not use fabric softener in washer or dryer.

2. From cream print fabric, cut 1 (17" x 72") strip. Turn each short raw end under ¼" twice and machine-stitch close to edge. With right sides together and raw edges aligned, fold strip in half lengthwise and stitch ¼" from edge along length of fabric. Turn right side out and press. Stitch 1" from seam line across length of strip to form inner ruffle.

3. Measure circumference of Styrofoam wreath. Divide by 2 and add ¼". Stitch across length of strip, using calculated measurement and working from last row of stitching, to make outer ruffle.

4. Using patterns, trace 11 hearts, 14 trees, 11 large stars, and 14 small stars onto paper side of Wonder-Under. Leaving approximate ½" margin, cut around Wonder-Under shapes. Press shapes onto wrong side of fabric scraps. Cut out shapes along pattern lines. Remove paper backing. Referring to photo, evenly space shapes and fuse onto outer ruffle, alternating hearts and trees; fuse large and small stars last. Keep 2 trees and 2 small stars aside for bow.

5. Using saw or knife, cut wreath widthwise at angle. Carefully gather fabric onto wreath. With hot-glue gun, glue cut ends back together. Let dry. Adjust fabric gathers to cover cut.

6. From red print fabric, cut 1 (6" x 45") strip. With right sides facing and raw edges aligned, fold strip in half lengthwise. Stitch ¼" from all edges, leaving opening for turning. Turn right side out and press. Slipstitch opening closed. Tie strip in bow. Referring to photo, center and fuse 1 tree and 1 small star to each tail of bow. Pin or stitch bow to wreath, covering where ruffle ends meet.

7. Sew plastic ring to wreath back for hanger.

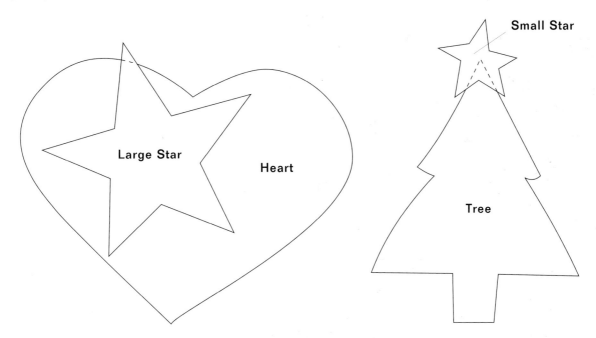

Dashed lines indicate underlying pattern pieces.

Charmed Stocking

Organdy pockets hold decorative treasures in this unusual stocking.

Materials

Tracing paper

1 yard white silk organdy

3/4"-wide Pellon® Wonder-Under® fusible tape

Assorted lightweight charms and beads

Copper fabric paint

Paintbrush

Ribbons: 1/2 yard 1/4"-wide, 1 yard 2 1/4"-wide wire-edged

Low temperature hot-glue gun and glue sticks

Small glass ornament (optional)

Instructions

1. Using patterns on page 32, trace and cut out stocking pattern. Using joined pattern, cut 3 stockings from organdy.

2. Cut Wonder-Under fusible tape into 7 (15"-long) strips. Cut strips in half widthwise to make narrower strips.

3. On 1 stocking piece, arrange Wonder-Under strips to form lattice pattern (see photo). Press each Wonder-Under strip onto stocking. (Each row of lattice strips will form pockets.) Remove paper backing from 1 row of lattice pockets, at sides and bottoms only, leaving paper backing at top of pockets. Align raw edges of second stocking piece with first, sandwiching fusible tape strips. Fuse 1 row of lattice pockets. Fill pockets with beads and charms as desired. (Do not fill pockets that are open on sides at this time.) Remove paper backing at top of pockets. Fuse pockets in place. Continue in this manner until desired number of pockets are filled.

4. To fill pockets along edges, insert beads and charms as desired. Cut fusible tape into 1" strips. Remove paper backing from fusible tape and insert web strips between top and bottom stocking layers. Fuse in place.

5. With fabric paint and paintbrush, embellish stocking with wavy lines along lattice pockets (see photo). Let dry.

6. To assemble stocking, press fusible tape along outer edge of remaining stocking piece. Cut notches into tape around curve of stocking foot. Remove paper backing. Place stocking with pockets faceup on top of remaining stocking, sandwiching Wonder-Under strips in between. Fuse in place. Trim edges. Paint edges with fabric paint (see photo). Let dry.

7. Fold edges down 1/4" along stocking top. Hot-glue in place. Cut 1/4"-wide ribbon in half lengthwise. Using 1 piece, fold ribbon in half to form loop. Referring to photo, hot-glue ribbon loop to top outer edge of stocking. Fold remaining piece in half and hot-glue center of ribbon next to loop ends, leaving ribbon ends free.

8. Gather 1 wire edge of ribbon by holding 1 end of wire and pulling other wire end through ribbon. Gather until ribbon fits around stocking top. Secure wire ends. Cut 1 ribbon end 1/2" over length needed. Fold ribbon raw edges under 1/4". Hot-glue raw edges in place. Hot-glue gathered ribbon to top outer edge of stocking.

9. If desired, tie ornament to stocking, using ends of hanging loop. Tie ends in bow.

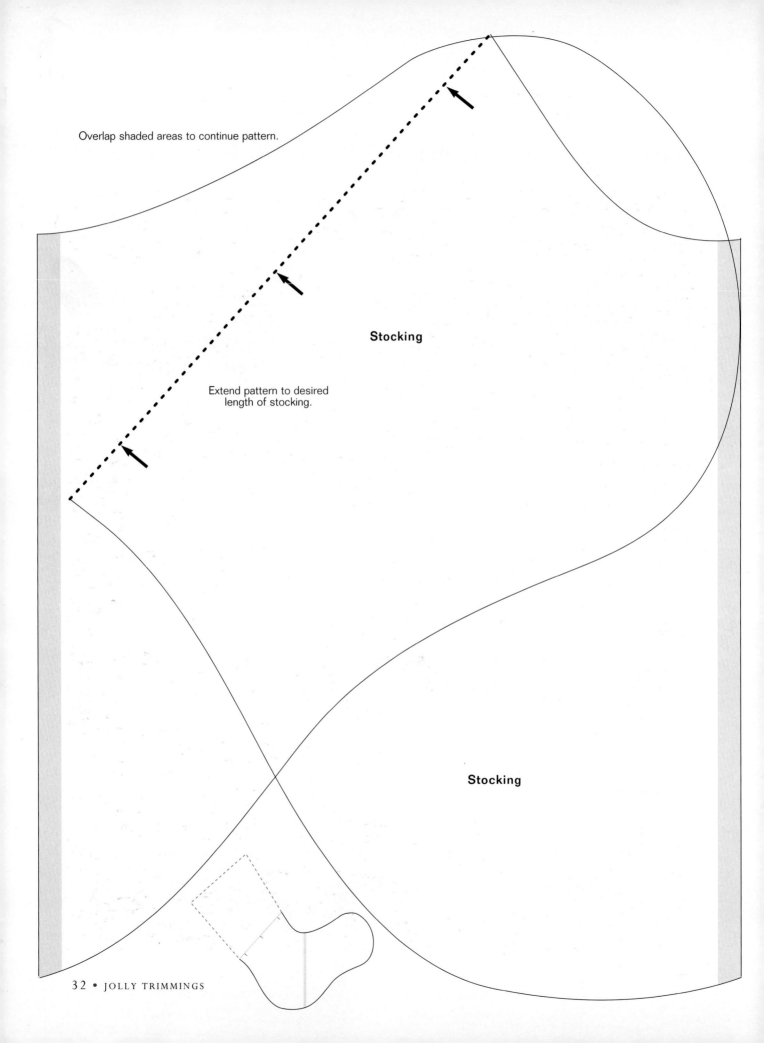

Overlap shaded areas to continue pattern.

Stocking

Extend pattern to desired
length of stocking.

Stocking

Scrappy Ornaments

These decorations are fun for kids to make and add homespun charm to your tree.

Materials (Makes 1 ornament.)

For each:

Pellon® Wonder-Under®

Fabric glue

Christmas Cone:

Construction paper or card stock

Assorted fabric scraps: green-and-
white prints, red-and-white prints

1½ yards ¼"-wide white ribbon

¾"-wide Pellon® Wonder-Under®
fusible tape

Compass

Hole punch

Snowman:

Assorted fabric scraps: white, black
gingham

Polyester stuffing

Black dimensional fabric paint in
squeeze bottle

Ribbons: 12"-length ⅜"-wide red
grosgrain, 8"-length ⅛"-wide
white satin

Carrot button

Reindeer:

Assorted fabric scraps: light brown,
dark brown

Card stock

½ yard ⅛"-wide green satin ribbon

Liquid ravel preventer

Polyester stuffing

Black thread

2 (¼") black buttons

Red pom-pom

Black dimensional fabric paint in
squeeze bottle

Christmas
Cone

Instructions

Christmas Cone

1. Cut construction paper into
1 (7") square. Cut 4 (1" x 7") strips
from green fabric and 3 (1" x 7")
strips from red fabric. Cut 6 (7")
lengths of white ribbon and 3 (7")
lengths of fusible tape. Cut each
fusible tape strip in half lengthwise.

2. Press Wonder-Under onto 1 side
of paper square. Remove paper
backing. Beginning with 1 green
fabric strip, alternate red and green
strips side by side until square is
covered. Fuse in place. Press fusible
tape strips to each ribbon length.
Remove paper backing. Fuse each
ribbon length to cover red-and-
green strip seams.

3. Place compass point at 1 corner
on wrong side of paper square.
Extend arm to adjacent corner.
Drag pencil across square to form

arc. Cut along line. Wrap cut piece
to form cone, with fabric side facing
out. Overlap edges and glue edges
in place. Let dry.

4. Punch holes at opposite sides of
cone near top edge. Insert remaining length of ribbon through holes;
double-knot ends to form hanger.

Snowman

1. Using patterns on page 35, trace
2 snowmen and 1 hat onto paper
side of Wonder-Under. Leaving
approximate ½" margin, cut around
Wonder-Under shapes. Press shapes
onto wrong side of fabric scraps.
Cut out shapes along pattern lines.
Remove paper backing from hat
only. Referring to photo, center and
fuse hat on right side of 1 snowman.
Remove paper backing from
remaining pieces.

2. Place snowman with hat faceup
on top of remaining snowman,
aligning raw edges. Fuse edges only,
leaving 2" opening for stuffing. Stuff
snowman to desired size. Fuse
opening closed.

3. Using dimensional fabric paint,
add 2 square eyes and paint 7 dots
for mouth on 1 side of snowman
(see photo). Let dry.

4. Tie red ribbon in bow. Trim ends.
Glue bow in place on hat and carrot
on face for nose. Let dry. Fold white
ribbon in half to form loop. Glue
both ends to center back at top of
snowman for hanger. Let dry.

Reindeer

1. Using patterns, trace 2 reindeer and 4 antlers onto paper side of Wonder-Under. Leaving approximate ½" margin, cut around Wonder-Under shapes. Press shapes onto wrong side of fabric scraps. Cut out shapes along pattern lines. Remove paper backing from antlers only. Fuse 1 pair of antlers to card stock. Cut card stock around antlers. Fuse remaining antlers to other side of card stock.

2. Cut 12 (1") lengths from green ribbon. Coat ribbon ends with liquid ravel preventer. Let dry.

3. Remove ½" of paper backing from 1 reindeer piece. Referring to photo, place ribbon pieces side by side halfway across top of reindeer piece. Remove remaining paper backing from both pieces. Stack remaining reindeer on top, sandwiching ribbon ends in between.

Fuse top edge in place. Press ribbon ends forward over top edges of reindeer. Continue fusing edges only, leaving 2" opening for stuffing. Stuff reindeer to desired size. Fuse opening closed.

4. Using black thread, sew 2 buttons on front of reindeer for eyes. Glue pom-pom in place for nose.

Fold green ribbon in half to form loop. Glue both ends to center back at top of reindeer for hanger. Let dry.

5. Using dimensional fabric paint, add 1 vertical line for mouth on 1 side of reindeer (see photo). Let dry.

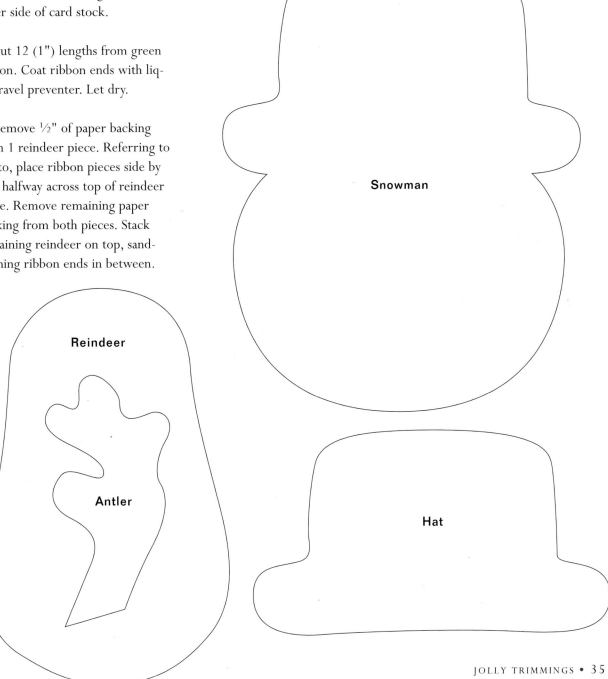

Snowman

Reindeer

Antler

Hat

Poinsettia Mantel Scarf

A table runner and a couple of napkins join together
to make the base of this merry mantel scarf.

Materials

72"-long purchased plain table
  runner
2 (16") purchased coordinating
  square napkins
Assorted fabric scraps for
  appliqués: red, green
¾"-wide Pellon® Wonder-Under®
  fusible tape
Pellon® Wonder-Under®
Thread: metallic gold, white
27 (15-mm) metallic gold beads
5 coordinating tassels

Instructions

1. Wash, dry, and iron table runner,
napkins, and fabrics. Do not use
fabric softener in washer or dryer.

2. Cut napkins in half diagonally. Set
1 triangle aside. Cut fusible tape to
equal 1 long edge of runner. Fuse

tape to wrong side of 1 long edge.
Remove paper backing. Referring to
photo, evenly space 3 napkin triangles faced down along 1 long edge
of runner (see Diagram), overlapping fusible tape and raw edges.
Fuse in place. Turn mantel scarf
right side up.

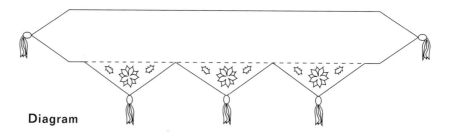

Diagram

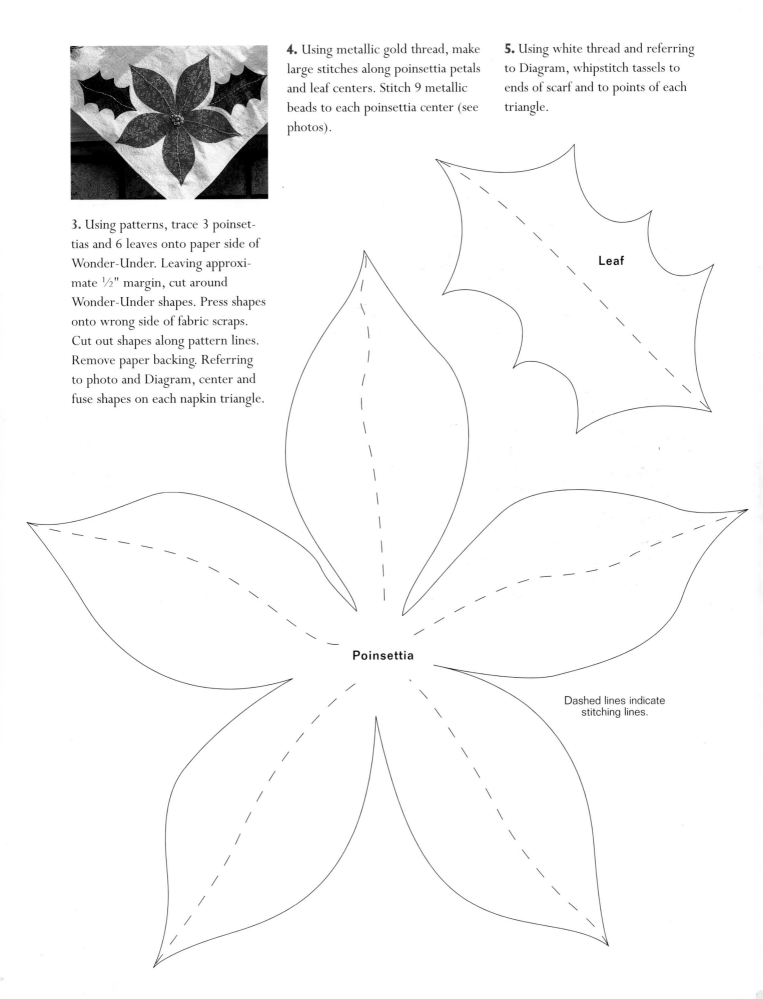

4. Using metallic gold thread, make large stitches along poinsettia petals and leaf centers. Stitch 9 metallic beads to each poinsettia center (see photos).

5. Using white thread and referring to Diagram, whipstitch tassels to ends of scarf and to points of each triangle.

3. Using patterns, trace 3 poinsettias and 6 leaves onto paper side of Wonder-Under. Leaving approximate ½" margin, cut around Wonder-Under shapes. Press shapes onto wrong side of fabric scraps. Cut out shapes along pattern lines. Remove paper backing. Referring to photo and Diagram, center and fuse shapes on each napkin triangle.

Leaf

Poinsettia

Dashed lines indicate stitching lines.

Sleeping Angels

Start a heavenly tradition by adding an angel to a child's blanket each year.

Materials

Purchased plain blanket

Fabrics: red, white, yellow, brown, and light brown scraps for appliqués; 5"-wide piece green felt

Pellon® Wonder-Under®

Invisible thread

White jumbo rickrack

Instructions

NOTE: If blanket will be washed frequently, outline motifs with coordinating dimensional fabric paint.

1. Wash, dry, and iron blanket and fabrics. Do not use fabric softener in washer or dryer.

2. Measure and cut green felt to fit blanket width. Cut Wonder-Under to fit width and length of green felt. Press Wonder-Under onto wrong side of felt. Remove paper backing. Referring to photo, position felt along top edge of wrong side of blanket. Fuse felt in place.

3. Using patterns, trace 3 wings, 3 heads, 3 hair pieces, and 3 dresses onto paper side of Wonder-Under. Leaving approximate ½" margin, cut around Wonder-Under shapes. Press shapes onto wrong side of fabric scraps. Cut out shapes along pattern lines. Remove paper backing. Referring to photo, center and fuse shapes on blanket, beginning with wings and ending with hair for each appliqué.

4. Starting at 1 short edge of green felt and using invisible thread, handstitch rickrack through all thicknesses, along all edges of green fabric. Overlap rickrack ends and knot thread when finished.

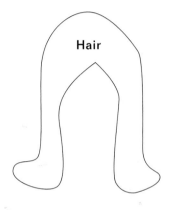

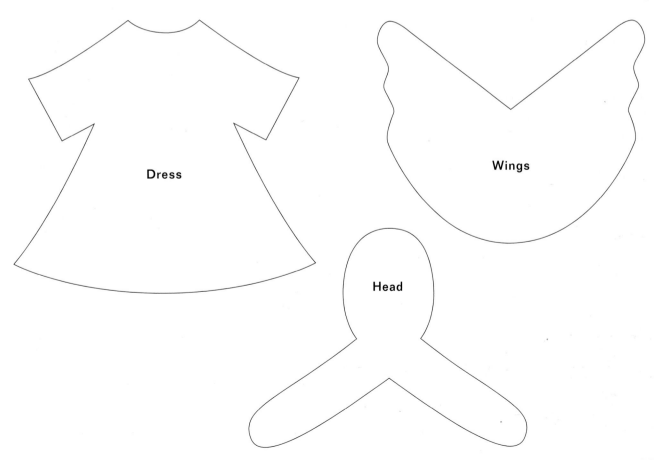

Stellar Night-light

This festive and functional light proves that the versatility of fusible web is endless.

Materials

2 (4" x 8" x ⅛") pieces balsa
Wood glue
Transparent tape
Pellon® Wonder-Under®
Craft knife
¼ yard sheer fabric
¾"-wide Pellon® Wonder-Under®
  fusible tape
¾ yard ½"-wide gold braid
Aluminum foil
Fabric glue
Night-light with power switch

Instructions

1. Place pieces of balsa together to form an 8" square. Glue pieces together at inner edges. Hold in place with tape until dry. Then remove tape.

2. Using pattern, trace 1 tree onto paper side of Wonder-Under; then trace 1 (8") square. Leaving approximate ½" margin, cut around Wonder-Under

shapes. Set aside Wonder-Under square; press tree onto 1 side of balsa square. Using craft knife, cut out tree from balsa. Cut inward from points of stars to prevent wood from splitting, trimming excess around tree last. Remove paper backing.

3. Cut 2 (8") squares from fabric. Press remaining Wonder-Under square to wrong side of 1 fabric square. Remove paper backing. Fuse fabric to blank side of wood. Fuse remaining sheer fabric square to opposite side of wood. Trim excess fabric around switch opening.

4. Cut fusible tape ½" wide. Press tape onto wrong side of braid. Remove paper backing. Starting at bottom, fuse braid to edges of night-light, covering raw edges of fabric. Rock iron back and forth to cover front and back edges. Fuse braid to inside edges of switch opening. (You can also glue braid to inside edge, if desired.)

5. Referring to pattern, cut triangle from aluminum foil. Center and glue to back of tree to shield tree from bulb heat and to increase reflection of light. Let dry. Center and glue night-light to back of finished tree. Let dry.

Cut out shaded areas.

Tree

Cut out shaded areas.

Switch opening

Fanciful Gifts

Photo Album, page 74

Breakfast Tray

Give a gift of treats in this delectable folding tray
made from napkins and cardboard.

Materials

Craft batting
Pellon® Wonder-Under®
2 (17") matching or contrasting
    square napkins
Brown fabric scrap for appliqués
White dimensional fabric paint in
    squeeze bottle
17"-square piece cardboard
Fabric glue
Red woven braid or trim
Red rickrack

Instructions

1. Cut 1 (16") square each from batting and Wonder-Under. Stack batting and Wonder-Under, with edges aligned, and press squares together. Remove paper backing. Place wrong side of 1 napkin onto Wonder-Under side of batting and fuse.

2. Using patterns, trace 6 gingerbread men and 4 hearts onto paper side of Wonder-Under. Leaving approximate ½" margin, cut around Wonder-Under shapes. Press shapes onto wrong side of fabric scraps. Cut out shapes along pattern lines. Remove paper backing. Referring to photo and alternating gingerbread men and hearts, center and fuse shapes on 2 opposite ends of batting-backed napkin, approximately 1" from napkin edges.

3. Outline gingerbread men and hearts along inner gray lines to resemble icing, using fabric paint. Let dry.

4. From cardboard, cut 1 (10") square and 4 (3" x 10") strips. Position pieces on wrong side of remaining napkin, centering 10" square and then surrounding square with 3" x 10" strips, with ¼" spaces between square and strips. Glue pieces to napkin with fabric glue. Let dry.

5. Cut 8 (10") lengths from red braid or trim for corner ties. On wrong side of batting, pin 1 end of each length, 3½" away from each corner (see Diagram). Stitch ends in place.

6. With wrong sides together and edges aligned, pin napkins together. Stitch napkins together along edges of cardboard square, stitching through ¼" spaces between square and strips (see Diagram). Place rickrack along outer edges of top napkin. Attach rickrack, stitching through all thicknesses and keeping corner ties free.

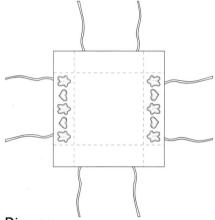

Diagram

7. To form tray, fold up sides. Gather corner ties and tie in bows. Turn corners out to reveal inner napkin if desired (see photo).

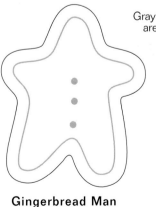

Gray lines and shaded
areas are painted.

Gingerbread Man

Heart

Crazy Quilt Jewelry

Transform scraps of ribbon into this stellar pin and necklace.

Materials (Makes 1 pin and 1 necklace.)

Craft paints: bronze, black, gold
Paintbrush
2 wooden star cutouts
Pellon® Wonder-Under®
Ribbons: assorted scraps, ⅝ yard ¼"-wide ribbon
Hot-glue gun and glue sticks
1 pin back
2" length narrow gold braid
1 (10-mm) jump ring

Instructions

1. Using bronze craft paint and paintbrush, apply paint to backs and edges of wooden stars. Let dry. Paint edges with black stripes. Let dry.

2. Press Wonder-Under onto wrong side of ribbon scraps. Combine 4 or 5 different ribbons to cover each wooden star. Cut ribbons to fit stars. Remove paper backing. Referring to photo, fuse ribbons to unpainted sides of stars, 1 piece at a time. Holding scissors at angle, trim excess ribbon from stars.

3. Hot-glue pin back to back of 1 star. Let dry.

4. Fold 2" length gold braid in half to make loop. Thread jump ring onto loop. Center jump ring on braid. Hot-glue loop ends underneath 1 ribbon point on remaining star. Let dry. Thread ¼"-wide ribbon through jump ring and knot ends for necklace.

5. Using gold craft paint, apply decorative painted lines where ribbons meet on front of each star (see photo). Let dry.

EXTRA: Experiment using other wooden cutouts. Most any shape will work, and fused fabric is a great alternative if you don't have ribbon handy. Using a much larger jump ring can easily turn a pendant into a key ring. Let children pick their own wooden cutouts and help them decorate their creations.

Photo Box

Dress up an ordinary shoe box and make an elegant haven for treasured snapshots.

Materials

Fabric*
Shoe box with lid
Pellon® Wonder-Under®
1½"-wide gold wire-edged ribbon*
Fabric glue
Wire twist tie

* Yardage will depend on size of shoe box.

Instructions

1. Remove lid from shoe box. Place box on wrong side of fabric. Measure height of box sides and add ¼". Beginning at bottom edge of box and using measurement, draw rectangle around box. Cut out rectangle. Reposition box in center of rectangle. Fold fabric up along edges of box. Mark edges and corners of box. Trim excess fabric from corners and edges, leaving ¼" for turning under on all edges. Press raw edges under ¼".

2. Place rectangle on paper side of Wonder-Under and trace. Cut out Wonder-Under shape along pattern lines. Press Wonder-Under shape onto wrong side of fabric. Remove paper backing. Referring to photo, fuse fabric to box bottom, sides, and ends. Repeat steps 1 and 2 for lid.

3. Measure 2 lengths of ribbon to equal length and width of lid, add 1" to each measurement, and then cut. Using fabric glue, attach ribbon ends to inside of box lid. Let dry. Tie bow with remaining ribbon (see diagrams 1–3). Center and glue bow on top of box lid. Let dry.

EXTRA: Pellon® Wonder-Under® doesn't bubble up like glue can. So go wild with your creativity and decorate your photo box with fabric, paper, trims, or color photocopies of favorite snapshots. Keep in mind that all the appliqué patterns found in this book can work on other projects. You can add light-bulb appliqués from the string-of-lights nightshirt (see page 106) and fuse the lights to the lid and sides of your photo box.

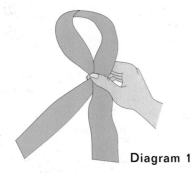

Diagram 1

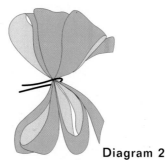

Diagram 2

Diagram 3

To make bow, measure 3" from end of ribbon. Pinch ribbon between thumb and forefinger. This is the center point of your bow. Make a 3" loop and pinch ribbon again at the center point (see Diagram 1). Twist ribbon at center and make a loop on opposite side. Continue with 4 more loops. Place twist tie over center of bow and fold in half (see Diagram 2). Holding ribbon loops firmly, twist wire until ribbon loops are tightly held together (see Diagram 3). Fluff bow by pulling firmly on loops. Trim excess from twist tie ends before gluing bow to box lid.

Seed Sachets

Need a quick gift idea? Cut pictures from magazines and seed catalogs or packages and fuse them to fabric pouches for sachets.

Materials (Makes 1 sachet.)
⅛ yard cream fabric
¾"-wide Pellon® Wonder-Under® fusible tape
Pellon® Wonder-Under®
Picture of flowers and corresponding seeds
Pinking shears
½ yard ⅛" nylon cord

Instructions
1. Cut fabric into 1 (6" x 12") strip. Cut fusible tape into 2 (6") lengths. Align each length of fusible tape to wrong side of fabric at each short raw edge. Press 1 fusible tape length to each raw edge. Remove paper backing. Fold down each Wonder-Under edge approximately 1", leaving ¼" at folded edge free from fusible tape. Fuse each folded edge.

2. Fold hemmed strip in half. Cut tape into 2 (5") lengths. Align raw fabric edge with tape. Press tape along 1 long side of fabric strip, 1" from hem. Repeat with remaining side. Remove paper backing. Fuse folded strip together at sides.

3. To embellish seed bag, press Wonder-Under onto wrong side of desired picture. Trim edges. Remove paper backing. Center and fuse picture on 1 side of bag (see photo).

4. To complete bag, trim side edges, using pinking shears. Thread nylon cord through casing at top of bag. Fill bag with seed. To close bag, pull cord ends.

EXTRA: Use the gift tag ideas (see page 57) in this chapter to add to your seed sachets. Complete the gift with growing instructions written on your personalized tag.

A Personal Initial

Help that privacy-minded teen claim her own space with a jumbo initial.

Materials

Purchased letter pattern*
Pellon® Wonder-Under®
Foam-core board
Fabric**
Fabric glue
1 yard 1"-wide ribbon
Hot-glue gun and glue sticks

* Look for house letters or alphabet stencils at home-improvement and art-supply stores. Enlarge chosen letter to desired size on photocopier.
** Yardage will depend on size of letter.

Instructions

1. Trace 2 of desired letter onto paper side of Wonder-Under. Cut out letters. Press 1 Wonder-Under letter onto 1 side of foam-core board and cut out along pattern lines. Remove paper backing. Fuse wrong side of fabric to board, sandwiching Wonder-Under in between. Trim fabric to within ½" from board edges. Fold excess fabric over edges. Glue in place with fabric glue. Let dry.

2. Press remaining letter to wrong side of remaining fabric. Cut fabric even with edges of letter. Remove paper backing. Fuse letter to back of remaining letter, covering raw edges of fabric.

3. Fold ribbon in half lengthwise and tie knot at center and at each end. Hot-glue knotted ends to corners of initial (see photo). Let dry.

EXTRA: Block letters work best when fusing fabric to foam-core board. But after you practice using these techniques, try scroll, cursive, or calligraphy-style lettering. Your kids can help decorate their initial, using colored paper and Pellon® Wonder-Under®. Hang the initial with ribbon or attach a picture hanger to the back with hot-glue for hanging on the wall.

Custom Gift Packages

Make your presents stand out from the crowd by placing them in custom-made fabric-covered containers.

Materials

For each:
Pellon® Wonder-Under®
Fabric*

Present Portfolio:
Purchased plain mailing envelope**
Liquid ravel preventer
Hot-glue gun and glue sticks
Trim or braid*
Velcro dots with adhesive backs

Gift Box:
Small box with lid***
Trim or ribbon*
Fabric glue

Fold-Up Box:
Thin cardboard
Liquid ravel preventer

* Yardage will depend on size of envelope or box used.
** Available at office-supply stores
*** Available at crafts stores

Instructions

Present Portfolio

1. Unfold mailing envelope and trace onto paper side of Wonder-Under. Press Wonder-Under onto wrong side of fabric and cut out along pattern lines. Remove paper backing. Fuse fabric to right side of mailing envelope. Trim edges. Apply liquid ravel preventer to all cut edges. Let dry.

2. Refold envelope and hot-glue along adjoining edges, keeping top flap free. Glue trim or braid to cut edges of envelope flap and seams (see photo). Let dry.

3. For portfolio closure, center and attach 1 Velcro dot set to flap and envelope.

Gift Box

1. Remove lid from box. Place box on wrong side of fabric. Measure height of box sides and add ¼". Beginning at bottom edge of box and using measurement, draw square around box. Cut out square. Reposition box in center of square. Fold fabric up along edges of box. Mark edges and corners of box. Trim excess fabric from corners and edges, leaving ¼" for turning under on all edges. Press raw edges under ¼".

2. Place square on paper side of Wonder-Under and trace. Cut out Wonder-Under shape along pattern lines. Press Wonder-Under shape onto wrong side of fabric. Remove paper backing. Referring to photo, fuse fabric to box bottom, sides, and ends. Repeat steps 1 and 2 for lid.

3. Measure 2 lengths of trim or ribbon to equal length and width of lid, add 1" to each measurement, and then cut. Using fabric glue, attach ends to inside of box lid. Let dry. Tie bow with remaining trim or ribbon. Center and glue bow on top of box lid. Let dry.

Fold-Up Box

1. Using pattern on page 56, trace pattern onto paper side of Wonder-Under. Press Wonder-Under onto 1 side of cardboard. Cut out cardboard along pattern lines. Remove paper backing. Fuse cardboard to wrong side of fabric. Trim around cardboard edges. Apply liquid ravel preventer to all cut edges. Let dry.

2. Score box fold lines into cardboard piece. Fold along lines, overlapping and underlapping edges to close.

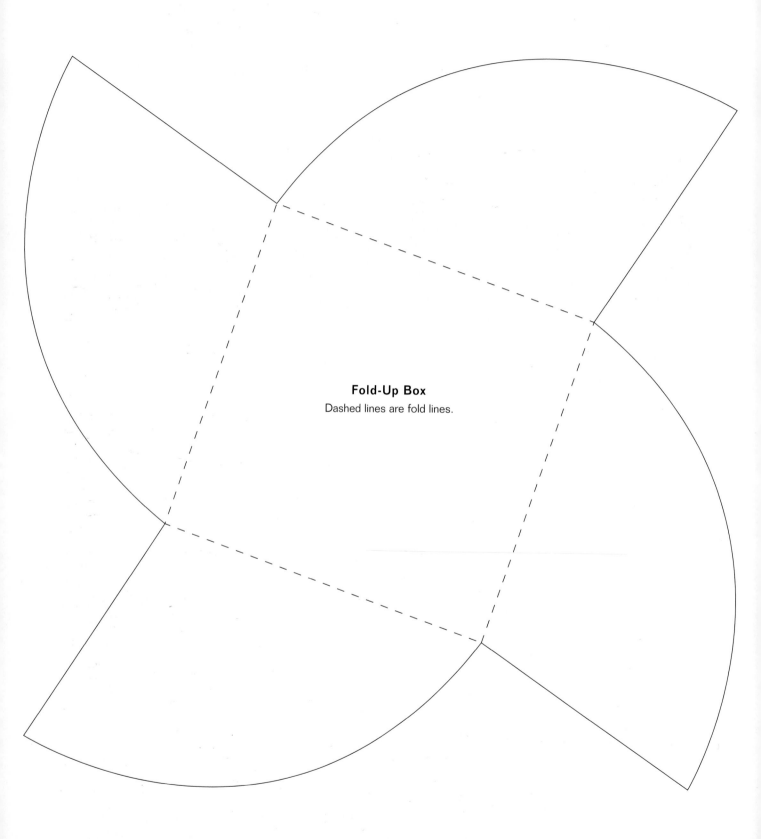

Fold-Up Box
Dashed lines are fold lines.

Handmade Gift Tags

Enhance even the most simply wrapped gifts with
gift tags made from scratch with scraps.

Materials

Pellon® Wonder-Under®
Assorted fabric scraps
Assorted card stock
Tracing paper
Craft glue
Assorted beads and sequins
Brass sheet metal and nail
Metallic gold thread
Gold paper clips (optional)
Assorted trims
⅛" hole punch
Assorted ribbons
Assorted dimensional fabric paint in
   squeeze bottles (optional)

Instructions

1. For nameplate, star, or circle tag, press Wonder-Under onto wrong side of desired fabric scrap. Remove paper backing. Fuse fabric to 1 side of card stock. Cut card-stock to desired shape and size.

For nameplate tag, cut small rectangle from brass sheet metal. Using nail, punch holes in metal to write name. Punch 1 hole in each corner of nameplate. With metallic thread, sew nameplate onto fabric-covered card stock.

For star tag, trace pattern onto tracing paper. Transfer pattern to sheet metal. Cut out star. With metallic thread, sew star onto fabric-covered card stock. Glue gold trim along tag edges. Let dry.

For circle tag, if desired, attach gold paper clips side by side along edge of fabric-covered card stock (see photo).

2. For diamond or tree tag, trace desired pattern onto paper side of Wonder-Under. Leaving approximate ½" margin, cut around Wonder-Under shape. Press shape onto wrong side of desired fabric scrap. Cut out shape along pattern lines. Remove paper backing. Referring to photo, fuse shape to card stock.

For diamond tag, trim excess fabric from center. Sew gold beads to outer edge of tag, using metallic thread and needle.

For tree tag, glue sequins to card front. Let dry.

3. For each tag, punch hole at center or corner of tag, using hole punch. Make hanger from desired trim or ribbon. Write name on tag, using dimensional fabric paint or pen. Let dry.

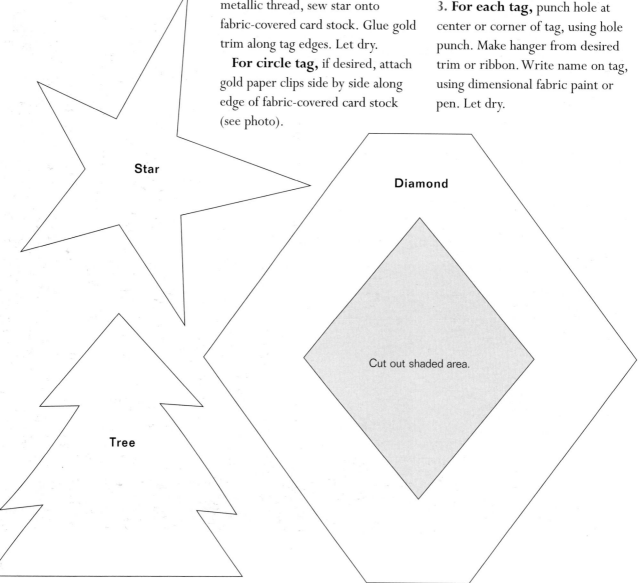

Star

Diamond

Cut out shaded area.

Tree

A Pet Project

Pay tribute to furry friends with "person"-alized wreath ornaments.

Materials (Makes 1 ornament.)

Pellon® Wonder-Under®

Assorted fabric scraps: green plaid, red print, tan

5"-square craft batting

Black dimensional fabric paint in squeeze bottle

12" length ⅛"-wide red ribbon

Fabric glue

Yellow embroidery floss

Instructions

1. Using patterns, trace 2 wreaths and 1 fish or 1 bone onto paper side of Wonder-Under. Leaving approximate ½" margin, cut around Wonder-Under shapes. Press shapes onto wrong side of green plaid fabric scraps. Cut out shapes along pattern lines. Remove paper backing. Referring to photo, center and fuse each wreath on 1 side of craft batting. Trim excess batting from inside edge and from around outside edges of wreath.

2. Press Wonder-Under onto wrong side of red print fabric scraps. Cut out desired number of ½"-diameter circles. Remove paper backing. Referring to photo, fuse red circles to 1 side of wreath; then fuse fish or bone to wreath.

3. Using dimensional fabric paint, write name of pet on fish or bone. Let dry.

4. Cut 4" length of ribbon. Tie ribbon in bow. Trim ends. Glue bow in place on fish or bone. Let dry. Fold remaining ribbon in half to form loop. Glue ends at top back of wreath for hanger. Let dry.

5. Using embroidery floss, blanket-stitch around inner and outer edge of wreath (see photo). Knot ends.

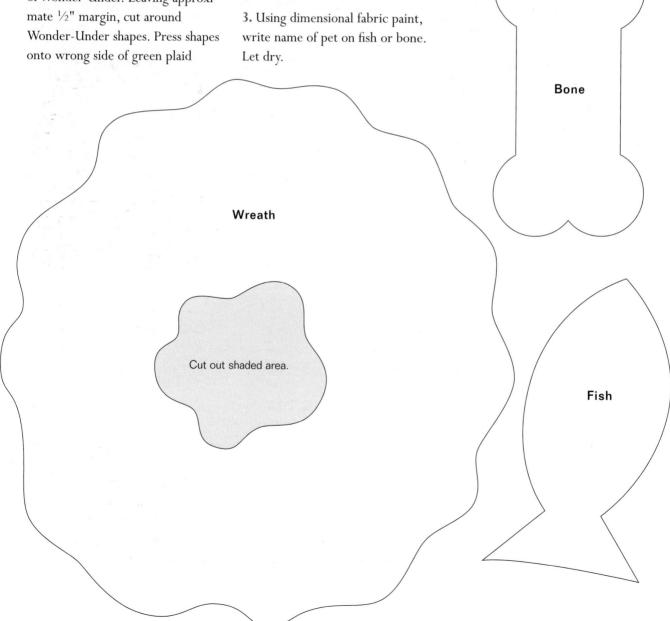

Bone

Wreath

Cut out shaded area.

Fish

Photo Wallet

Insert a few photographs of your own when giving this portable brag book.

Materials

2 plastic sheet protectors
2 (6" x 24") strips fuchsia
   Ultrasuede®
Transparent tape
Fuchsia thread
Pellon® Wonder-Under®
1 yard 1"-wide coordinating
   grosgrain ribbon
Fabric glue

Instructions

1. Cut 5 (3¾" x 5½") pieces from plastic sheet protectors. Beginning 1½" from 1 short edge of 1 Ultrasuede piece, position plastic pieces along right side of Ultrasuede, leaving ½" between each piece. Tape each piece in place to prevent shifting. Edgestitch along edges and bottoms of plastic pieces. Remove tape.

2. Press Wonder-Under onto wrong side of remaining Ultrasuede piece. Remove paper backing. Stack both Ultrasuede strips, with wrong sides together, sandwiching Wonder-Under in between. Fuse pieces together. Trim edges evenly, if necessary.

3. Fold up bottom of wallet, beginning at bottom edge and folding inward toward plastic pockets. Center and glue ribbon center to back of wallet. Let dry. Tie ribbon in bow around wallet to close. Trim ends of ribbon at angle.

Pencil Toppers

Craft these felt adornments in multiples for best chums and school bazaars.

Materials

For each:

Tracing paper

Pencil

Red felt scraps

Pellon® Wonder-Under®

Fabric glue

Fine-tip permanent black fabric
   marker

Soldier:

Assorted felt scraps: blue, black,
   light peach

2 (8-mm) wiggle eyes

4 (¼") yellow pom-poms

Elf:

Assorted felt scraps: light peach,
   green

2 (8-mm) wiggle eyes

Pom-poms: 1 (¼") yellow, 3 (¼")
   green

Reindeer:

Assorted felt scraps: green, light
   tan

2 (6-mm) wiggle eyes

1 (½") red pom-pom

Instructions

Soldier

1. Using patterns on page 64, trace 1 soldier head, 1 soldier face, 1 soldier hair, 1 reversed soldier hair, and 1 soldier hat brim onto tracing paper. Cut out patterns. Cut 2 soldier heads from blue felt. Trace remaining patterns onto paper side of Wonder-Under. Leaving approximate ½" margin, cut around Wonder-Under shapes. Press shapes onto 1 side of felt scraps. Cut out shapes along pattern lines. Remove paper backing. Referring to photo, fuse shapes 1–3, in that order, to 1 soldier head.

2. Using fabric glue, attach wiggle eyes to soldier face. Let dry. With fabric marker, draw mouth and 2 lines on soldier hat (see photo). Glue 1 yellow pom-pom at each end of each line. Let dry.

3. Stack finished head faceup on remaining soldier head. Glue along all edges except bottom. Let dry. Insert pencil into bottom edge.

Elf

1. Using patterns on page 65, trace 1 elf head, 1 elf face, and 1 elf hatband onto tracing paper. Cut out patterns. Cut 2 elf heads from red felt. Trace remaining patterns onto paper side of Wonder-Under. Leaving approximate ½" margin, cut around Wonder-Under shapes. Press shapes onto 1 side of felt scraps. Cut out shapes along pattern lines. Remove paper backing. Referring to photo, fuse shapes 1 and 2, in that order, to 1 elf head.

2. Using fabric glue, attach wiggle eyes to elf face. Let dry. With fabric marker, draw mouth. Glue yellow pom-pom at hat point. Let dry. Evenly space and glue green pom-poms along elf collar. Let dry.

3. Stack finished head faceup on remaining elf head. Glue along all edges except bottom. Let dry. Insert pencil into bottom edge.

Reindeer

1. Using patterns on page 65, trace 1 reindeer head, 1 reindeer face, and 1 bow onto tracing paper. Cut out patterns. Cut 2 reindeer heads from green felt. Trace remaining patterns onto paper side of Wonder-Under. Leaving approximate ½" margin, cut around

Wonder-Under shapes. Press shapes onto 1 side of felt scraps. Cut out shapes along pattern lines. Remove paper backing. Referring to photo, fuse shapes 1 and 2, in that order, to 1 reindeer head.

2. Using fabric glue, attach wiggle eyes to reindeer face. Let dry. With fabric marker, draw mouth. Glue red pom-pom to reindeer face for nose. Let dry.

3. Stack finished head faceup on remaining reindeer head. Glue along all edges except bottom. Let dry. Insert pencil into bottom edge.

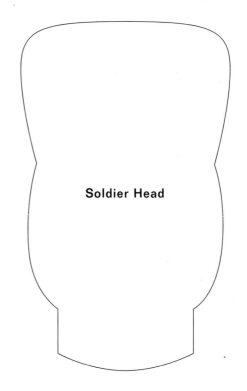

Soldier Head

Soldier Face
1

Soldier Hat Brim
3

Soldier Hair
Trace. Reverse and
trace again.

2

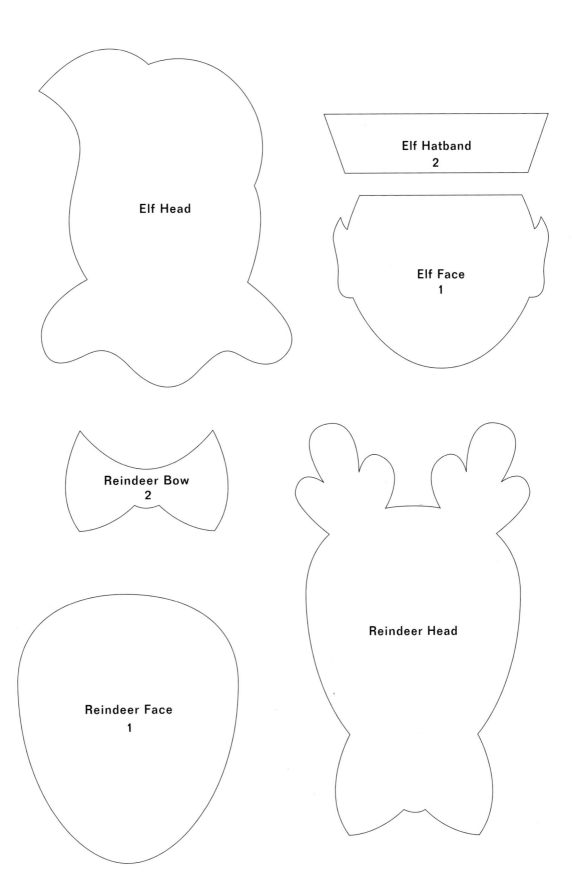

Elf Head

Elf Hatband
2

Elf Face
1

Reindeer Bow
2

Reindeer Head

Reindeer Face
1

Family Calendar

Delight an out-of-town relative with this calendar that features family photos celebrating the previous year month by month.

Materials

12 color photos

12 (11" x 17") sheets card stock

Pellon® Wonder-Under®

Assorted fabric scraps for appliqués

Permanent markers in desired colors

Instructions

NOTE: Our patterns and instructions represent the photographed samples. Use these instructions along with patterns of your choice to create your unique calendar.

1. Photocopy 12 desired photos, using a color copier. On sheets of card stock, photocopy the calendar page on page 68. You can choose to photocopy the months provided on page 69 or write them (see Step 4).

2. **For watermelon, football, or star calendar page,** using patterns, trace desired number of motifs onto paper side of Wonder-Under. Leaving approximate ½" margin, cut around Wonder-Under shapes. Press shapes onto wrong side of fabric scraps. Cut out shapes along pattern lines. Remove paper backing and set aside.

3. Cut 1 (7¼" x 10½") rectangle from Wonder-Under. Press onto wrong side of desired fabric and cut out. Remove paper backing. Center and fuse fabric on upper half of calendar page. Trace 1 photocopy onto paper side of Wonder-Under. Cut out Wonder-Under. Press Wonder-Under onto wrong side of photocopy. Remove paper backing. Center and fuse photocopy on fabric square. Fuse desired motifs along edges of rectangle and photocopy.

4. If desired, write and fill in months and dates for the upcoming year, using markers.

EXTRA: When your calendar is complete, go back to the copy center to have the calendar bound. Or punch 2 holes at the top and hang the calendar pages on adjustable rings.

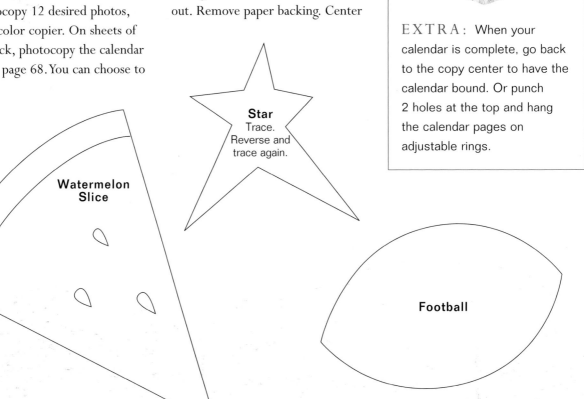

Watermelon Slice

Star
Trace.
Reverse and
trace again.

Football

Sunday	Monday	Tuesday	Wednesday	Thursday	Friday	Saturday

January

February

March

April

May

June

July

August

September

October

November

December

Fabric Fun Stickers

To make your own Christmas stickers,
combine common stick-on labels and fabric cutouts.

Materials

Pellon® Wonder-Under®
Assorted fabric scraps for
  appliqués
½"-wide white self-adhesive labels
Fine-tip permanent black marker
  (optional)

Instructions

1. Using patterns, trace desired
motifs onto paper side of Wonder-
Under. Leaving approximate ½"
margin, cut around Wonder-Under
shapes. Press shapes onto wrong
side of fabric scraps. Cut out shapes
along pattern lines. Remove paper
backing. Referring to photos, fuse
1 shape onto each label. (Use dry
iron to apply fusible web to labels,
and you won't disturb adhesive.)

2. If desired, use marker to embellish shapes with drawn stitches
(see photos). Decorate labels with
chosen motifs or make stickers from
motifs by trimming around edge of
each motif (see photo).

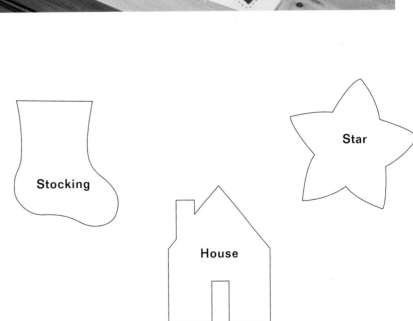

Tree

Stocking

House

Star

Earring Screen

This colorful earring organizer holds numerous pairs and packs flat for travel.

Materials

Pellon® Wonder-Under®

Ribbons: 3 yards 1¾"-wide, 2½ yards ⅜"-wide, ⅓ yard 1¾"-wide

2 (8" x 10") precut mats

Fabric glue

2 (8" x 10") pieces of vinyl screen

Instructions

1. Press Wonder-Under onto wrong side of 1¾"-wide ribbon. Cut ribbon into 4 (12") lengths and 4 (10") lengths. Remove paper backing. Referring to photo, fuse 12" ribbon lengths to sides of 1 precut mat and then fuse 10" ribbon lengths to top and bottom or mat. Turn ribbon ends under and fuse to back of mat.

Repeat with remaining mat. Fuse remaining 1¾"-wide ribbon to inside top edge of 1 mat. Cut ends flush with mat.

2. On wrong side of 1 mat, glue 1 screen piece to inside edges. Let dry. Repeat with remaining screen piece. Let dry.

3. To embellish holder, glue strips of ⅜"-wide ribbon along edges of earring holder (see photo). Let dry. Stack mats with wrong sides together. To create top hinge, cut 2 (14") lengths from remaining ⅜"-wide ribbon. Glue ribbon onto edge of earring holder, extending ends over mat edges. Let dry.

4. To connect mats at bottom edges, cut ⅓ yard of ribbon into 2 (6") lengths. Glue 1 end of 1 length to inside bottom edge of mat. Let dry. Repeat with remaining length and other bottom edge. Connect remaining end of each to inside of bottom mat. Glue and let dry.

EXTRA: Precut mats come in all shapes and sizes. Try an oval or a square. You'll see that the varieties of mats allow you to make several gifts—each unique—using the same techniques.

Photo Album

Small photo albums make great momentos of Christmas festivities. Insert instant photos taken at a party and then let each guest take an album home.

Materials

Cardboard
10 precut postcard-sized art papers
Fabric
Pellon® Wonder-Under®
2 (⅛"-diameter) metal eyelets with eyelet tool
¼" hole punch
½ yard ⅜"-wide grosgrain ribbon
Construction paper: red, green
Gold paint pen
Hot-glue gun and glue sticks
Gold charm

Instructions

1. Cut 2 pieces from cardboard, ½" larger all around than precut postcards. Cut 2 pieces from fabric, ¾" larger than cardboard pieces; then cut 2 pieces, ⅛" smaller than cardboard pieces. Set aside.

2. Press Wonder-Under onto wrong side of all fabric pieces. Remove paper backing. Referring to photo, fuse large fabric pieces to 1 side of each cardboard piece. Fold fabric to back of each cardboard piece and fuse in place. Center and fuse small fabric pieces to back of cardboard pieces to cover raw edges.

3. Following manufacturer's instructions, punch 2 eyelets in 1 short end of each cardboard piece. Matching distance between eyelets, use hole punch to punch 2 holes in 1 short end of postcard stack.

4. Cut ribbon in half. For each hole, thread 1 length through front cardboard, postcards, and back cardboard (see photo). Tie ribbon in bow.

5. Embellish front album cover with rectangles cut from construction paper. Outline edges with gold paint. Let dry. Hot-glue charm to center of album. Let dry.

EXTRA: When tying ribbons on your album, leave slack for the photos that will be added later. Otherwise, you may have to adjust the bows after every addition.

Seasonal Fashions

Happy Snowman Dress, page 82

Twinkling Tree Scarf

Branch out and decorate this soft wrap with star-topped trees.

Materials

Assorted felt scraps for appliqués:
  dark green, light green, yellow
Pellon® Heavy Duty Wonder-Under®
Purchased plain scarf or 12" x 72"
  polar fleece piece with 4"-long
  fringe at each end

Instructions

NOTE: If scarf will be washed frequently, outline motifs with coordinating dimensional fabric paint or blanket-stitch around appliqués.

1. Wash, dry, and iron scarf and fabrics. Do not use fabric softener in washer or dryer.

2. Using patterns, trace 4 large trees, 4 small trees, 4 large stars, and 4 small stars onto paper side of Wonder-Under. Leaving approximate ½" margin, cut around Wonder-Under shapes. Press shapes onto wrong side of felt scraps. Cut out shapes along pattern lines. Remove paper backing. Referring to photo, center and fuse shapes on each end of scarf above fringe, beginning with trees and then adding stars.

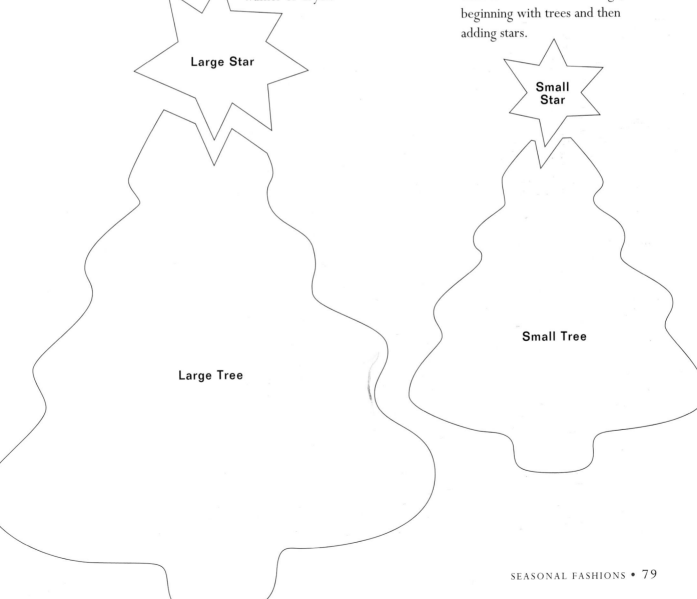

Large Star

Small Star

Large Tree

Small Tree

Night on the Town

Glittery fabric ornaments turn this
purchased vest into a festive favorite.

Materials

Pellon® Heavy Duty Wonder-Under®
Sequined fabric scraps for
  appliqués: blue, red, purple, gold
Liquid ravel preventer
Purchased plain vest
2 yards each gold metallic ribbons:
  ⅛"-wide, 1½"-wide
Gold thread

Instructions

1. Using pattern, trace 4 ornaments
onto paper side of Wonder-Under.
Leaving approximate ½" margin,
cut around Wonder-Under shapes.
Press shapes onto wrong side of fabric scraps. Cut out shapes along pattern lines. Remove paper backing.
Apply liquid ravel preventer to cut
edges. Let dry. Referring to photo,
fuse shapes to vest front.

2. Referring to photo, for each
ornament, measure 1 (⅛"-wide)
ribbon length that extends from
shoulder seams to top of ornament,
add 2" to measurement, and then
cut. Apply liquid ravel preventer to
cut ends. Let dry. With gold thread,
handstitch each ribbon end in place
at shoulder seam. Twist each ribbon
loosely and stitch in place at top of
corresponding ornament.

3. Cut 1½"-wide ribbon into
4 equal lengths. Tie each length in
bow. Handstitch 1 bow to top of
each ornament, covering end of
twisted ribbon.

Ornament

Happy Snowman Dress

This cheery dress will bring a twinkle to your girl's eyes.

Materials

Purchased plain dress
Assorted fabric scraps for
    appliqués: white-on-white print,
    green, red-and-green plaid,
    yellow print, cream Christmas
    print, light pink print
Pellon® Wonder-Under®
Black pearl cotton
3 (³⁄₈") red buttons

Instructions

1. Wash, dry, and iron dress and fabrics. Do not use fabric softener in washer or dryer.

2. Using patterns, trace 7 small stars, 3 large stars, 1 snowman, 1 coat, 1 muffler, 1 earmuff band, 1 nose, and 1 of each earmuff, glove, and heart onto paper side of Wonder-Under. Leaving approximate ½" margin, cut around Wonder-Under shapes. Press shapes onto wrong side of fabric scraps.

Cut out shapes along pattern lines. Remove paper backing. Referring to photo, fuse shapes 1–9, in that order, to dress front. Randomly fuse stars around snowman and on pockets.

3. With black pearl cotton, edgestitch around all appliqués. Make French knots for snowman eyes and stitch curve for snowman mouth. Stitch buttons down front of snowman coat.

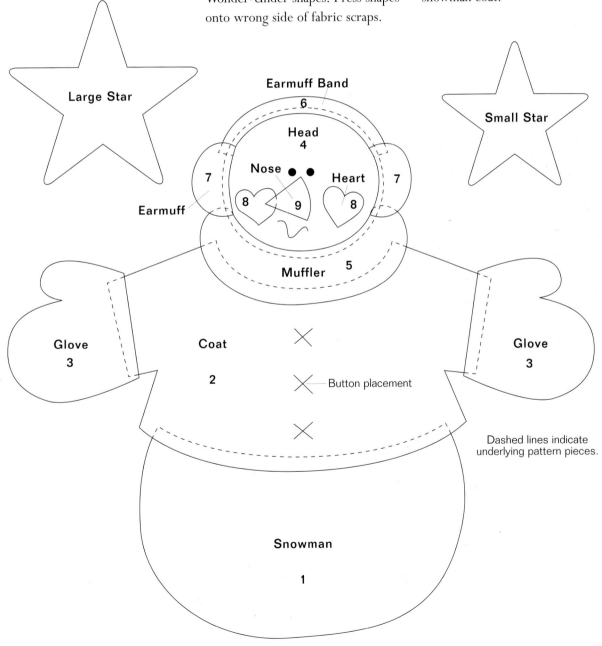

Christmas Sampler Sweatshirt

In a matter of minutes, you can whip up a seasonal sweatshirt that puts familiar icons front and center.

Materials

Purchased plain sweatshirt

Assorted fabric scraps for appliqués: green, red-and-green plaid

Pellon® Wonder-Under®

Tear-away stabilizer

Thread: green, cream

⅝ yard ¼"-wide metallic gold braid

Liquid ravel preventer

⅝ yard ⅜"-wide cream gold-edged ribbon

3 (½") gold star-shaped buttons

Instructions

1. Wash, dry, and iron sweatshirt and fabrics. Do not use fabric softener in washer or dryer.

2. Using patterns, trace 3 trees, 3 stockings, 3 cuffs, and 3 wreaths onto paper side of Wonder-Under. Leaving approximate ½" margin, cut around Wonder-Under shapes. Press shapes onto wrong side of fabric scraps. Cut out shapes along pattern lines. Remove paper backing. Referring to photo, center and fuse shapes on sweatshirt front.

3. Following manufacturer's instructions, attach tear-away stabilizer to inside of sweatshirt front. Satin-stitch around appliqués, using sewing machine and green thread.

4. Referring to photo for length, cut 2 lengths of gold braid. Apply liquid ravel preventer to cut ends. Let dry. Machine-stitch through middle of each braid length, using cream thread.

5. Cut ribbon into 3 equal lengths. Tie each length in bow. Handstitch 1 bow to bottom of each wreath. Sew 1 star button to top of each tree.

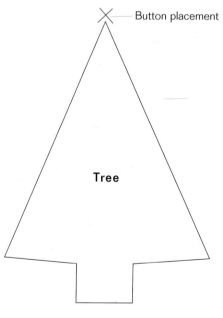

× — Button placement

Tree

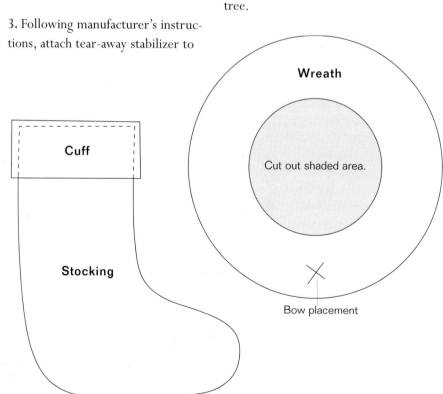

Cuff

Stocking

Wreath

Cut out shaded area.

× Bow placement

Snowy Village Jumper

Buttons, beads, and fabric scraps turn an ordinary
purchased jumper into a winter wonderland.

Materials

Purchased plain jumper

Fabrics: blue print, gold print, light gray print, 2 light and 1 dark green print, and 1 red solid and 2 red print scraps; ½ yard white-on-white print; ¼ yard each yellow, 2 light brown prints, and 1 dark brown print; ⅛ yard each 3 light brown stripe

Pellon® Wonder-Under®

Rotary cutter with wavy blade

Thread: white, red, green

3 (¼" to ½") white buttons

Assorted seed beads

Needlenose pliers (optional)

Assorted Christmas buttons or charms

Fine-tip permanent black fabric marker

Gold embroidery floss

Instructions

1. Wash, dry, and iron jumper and fabrics. Do not use fabric softener in washer or dryer.

2. Trace 3 (4½" x 5½") rectangles onto paper side of Wonder-Under. *(Note:* These rectangles are each pattern piece 2.) Using patterns on pages 88–90, trace 3 front steps, 1 side chimney, 1 reversed side chimney, 1 side chimney snow, 1 reversed side chimney snow, 1 chimney, 1 chimney snow, 3 roofs, 3 roof snows, 2 trees, 7 hedges, 7 hedge snows, 3 birds, 3 bird beaks, 1 house A, 1 house B, 1 house C, 1 door D, 1 door E, 1 door F, 2 large stars, 2 small stars, 2 wide trees, and 2 thin trees onto paper side of Wonder-Under. Leaving approximate ½" margin, cut around Wonder-Under shapes.

Press shapes onto wrong side of fabric scraps. Cut out shapes along pattern lines. Using rotary cutter and wavy blade and referring to pattern, cut each roof into 3 pieces. Remove paper backing. Referring to photo, center and fuse shapes 1–18, in that order, to bottom of jumper front.

3. Using white thread, sew buttons on door fronts for doorknobs. Using red or green thread, sew seed beads on trees. With needlenose pliers, break off shanks from buttons if necessary; then sew buttons or charms to house windows and front doors, using red or green thread.

4. Using fabric marker, draw 1 black dot for bird eye on each bird. With embroidery floss and needle, stitch 2 long straight stitches for each pair of bird legs.

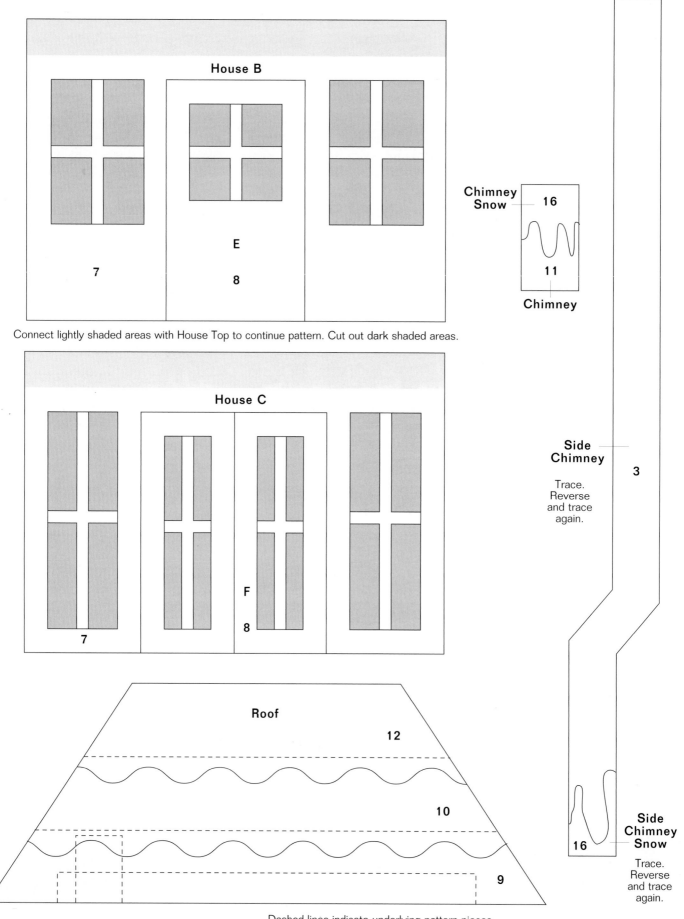

House B

E

7

8

Connect lightly shaded areas with House Top to continue pattern. Cut out dark shaded areas.

House C

F

7

8

Roof

12

10

9

Dashed lines indicate underlying pattern pieces.

Chimney Snow 16

11

Chimney

Side Chimney

Trace. Reverse and trace again.

3

Side Chimney Snow 16

Trace. Reverse and trace again.

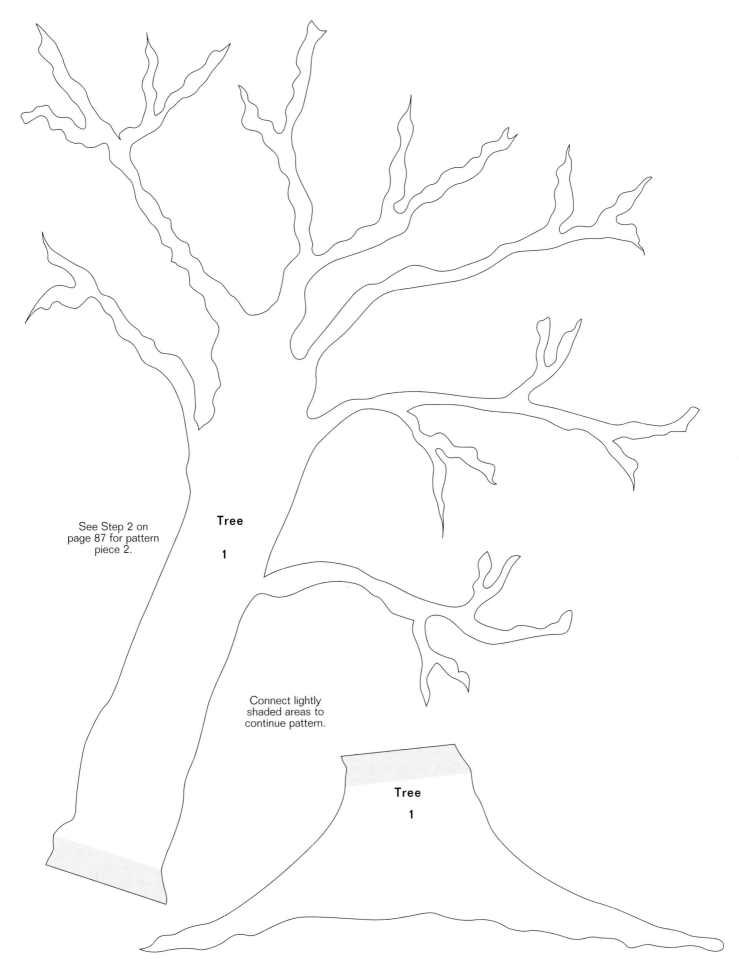

See Step 2 on page 87 for pattern piece 2.

Tree

1

Connect lightly shaded areas to continue pattern.

Tree

1

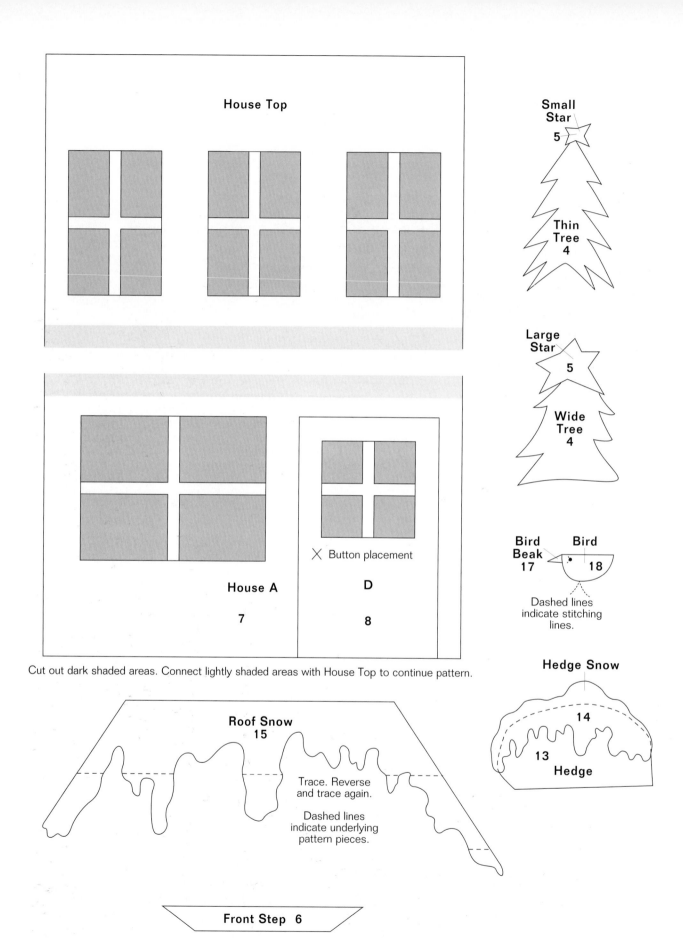

House Top

Small Star
5

Thin Tree
4

Large Star
5

Wide Tree
4

House A
7

D
8

✕ Button placement

Bird Beak
17

Bird
18

Dashed lines indicate stitching lines.

Cut out dark shaded areas. Connect lightly shaded areas with House Top to continue pattern.

Hedge Snow

14

13

Hedge

Roof Snow
15

Trace. Reverse and trace again.

Dashed lines indicate underlying pattern pieces.

Front Step 6

Beary Plaid Romper

Recycle scraps from your toddler's outgrown clothes for the appliqués on this outfit.

Materials

Purchased plain romper
Assorted fabric scraps for
    appliqués: brown, cream,
    Christmas plaid
Pellon® Wonder-Under®
Dimensional fabric paints in
    squeeze bottles: green, black
Black thread
2 (¼") black shank buttons
    (optional)

Instructions

NOTE: Button eyes are suggested for this project, but French knots are recommended for children's clothing to prevent a possible hazard.

1. Wash, dry, and iron romper and fabrics. Do not use fabric softener in washer or dryer.

2. Using patterns below and on page 93, trace 1 bear, 1 bear nose, 1 tree, and 1 overalls onto paper side of Wonder-Under. Leaving approximate ½" margin, cut around Wonder-Under shapes. Press shapes onto wrong side of fabric scraps. Cut out shapes along pattern lines. Remove paper backing. Referring to photo, center and fuse shapes to romper front.

3. Using green fabric paint, outline bear, tree, and overalls. Let dry. Using black fabric paint, draw nose and mouth. Let dry.

4. With black thread, sew buttons to bear face for eyes if desired or make French knots.

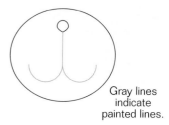

Gray lines
indicate
painted lines.

Bear Nose

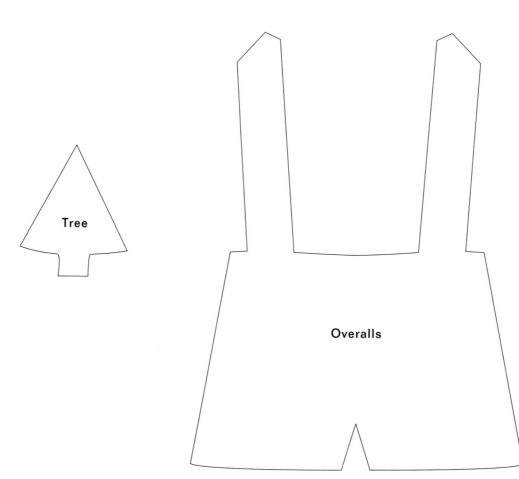

Tree

Overalls

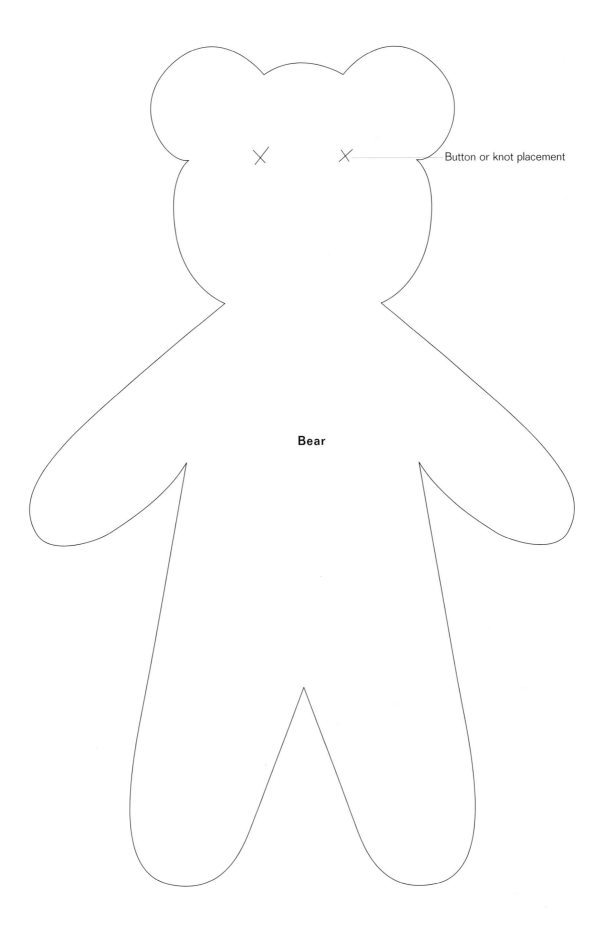

Button or knot placement

Bear

Napkin Apron

Three purchased napkins and crisp white appliqués
come together to deck you out in holiday charm.

Materials

3 (18") square napkins
White fabric scraps for appliqués
Pellon® Wonder-Under®
¾"-wide Pellon® Wonder-Under®
    fusible tape
10 (¾") buttons
Green thread

Instructions

NOTE: If apron will be washed frequently, outline motifs with coordinating dimensional fabric paint.

1. Wash, dry, and iron napkins and fabric. Do not use fabric softener in washer or dryer.

2. Using patterns on page 95, trace 2 short trees, 2 tall trees, 2 stars, and 1 man onto paper side of Wonder-Under. Leaving approximate ½" margin, cut around Wonder-Under shapes. Press shapes onto wrong side of fabric scraps. Cut out shapes along pattern lines. Remove paper backing. Referring to photo, center and fuse shapes along lower edge of 1 napkin. Set aside.

3. Press Wonder-Under tape onto 1 edge of second napkin. Then cut 3 (9") strips of tape. Referring to

Assembly Diagram, evenly space strips vertically along lower edge of napkin and press, beginning at Wonder-Under edge. Remove paper backing. Referring to Assembly Diagram, place Napkin 1 right side up on top of Napkin 2. With side edges aligned, fuse napkins together.

4. From remaining napkin, cut off hemmed edges. Set aside for neck and waist ties. If desired, machine-zigzag cut edges of ties. Cut napkin into 13" square. Press fusible tape along 3 edges of napkin. Remove paper backing. Fold along edge of tape pieces to hem; fuse. Place square right side up. Press fusible tape along unhemmed edge. Remove paper backing. Referring to Assembly Diagram, place top edge

of Napkin 2 on botton edge of Napkin 3 square, sandwiching Wonder-Under. Fuse in place.

5. Referring to Assembly Diagram, place neck and waist ties at top corners of apron top and bottom. Sew buttons at these corners to attach ties (see photo). Sew remaining buttons to corners and along center where 2 bottom napkins meet to form pockets (see photo).

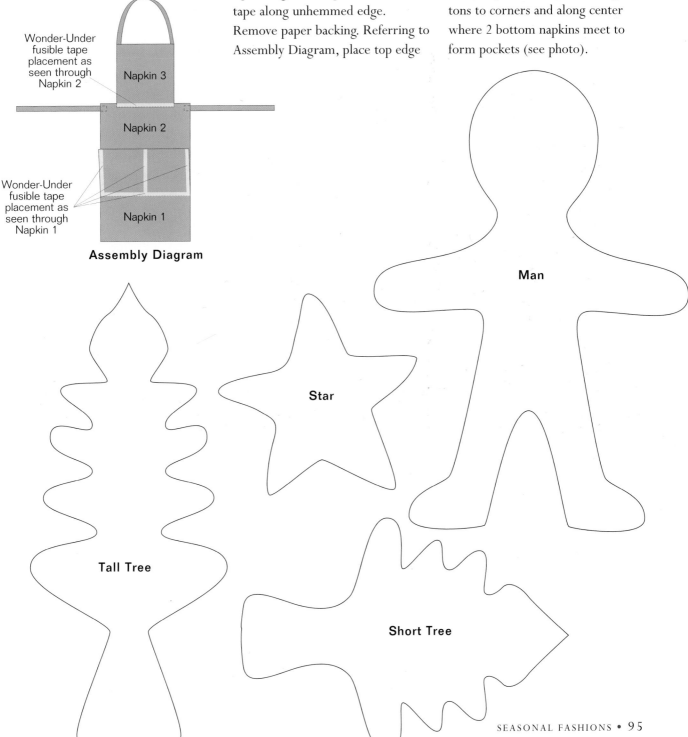

Wonder-Under fusible tape placement as seen through Napkin 2

Napkin 3

Napkin 2

Wonder-Under fusible tape placement as seen through Napkin 1

Napkin 1

Assembly Diagram

Tall Tree

Star

Man

Short Tree

Christmas Tree Dress

How easy can you get? Buttons and polka-dot ribbons
create quick holiday delight on this sweatshirt dress.

Materials

Purchased plain sweatshirt dress
Ribbons for appliqués: 1 yard
   ⅝"-wide green-and-white dot
   grosgrain, 3" (1½"-wide) red-and-
   white dot grosgrain
¾"-wide Pellon® Wonder-Under®
   fusible tape
White dimensional fabric paint
White thread
Buttons: 6 red heart-shaped,
   9 yellow star-shaped

Instructions

1. Wash, dry, and iron dress and
ribbons. Do not use fabric softener
in washer or dryer.

2. Trim fusible tape to fit ribbon
widths. Press tape onto wrong side
of all ribbon pieces. Cut green ribbon into 8", 6½", 5", 3½", and 2"
lengths. Cut green and red ribbon
ends at angle. Remove paper backing. Referring to photo for position-
ing, center and fuse ribbon lengths
to dress front, leaving ¾" between
each ribbon. Center and fuse red
ribbon ½" under tree.

3. Using fabric paint, cover raw
edges of ribbon pieces. Let dry.

4. Sew buttons onto dress front,
using white thread and alternating
hearts and stars between
ribbons (see photo).

EXTRA: Use ribbon
scraps to make other
Christmas motifs. Straight-
edged designs, such as gift
packages, stars (see the table
runner on page 122), and
funky geometric ornaments,
can fill up a sweatshirt front.

Holiday Bibs

These beautifully useful bibs show the spirit of the season on bears—or babies!

Materials (Makes 1 bib.)

Mouse:

Pellon® Wonder-Under®

Fabric scraps for appliqués: gray
  print, 2 red prints, green-and-red
  print, green print

Purchased plain bib

Powdered blush and brush
  (optional)

Fine-tip permanent black fabric
  marker

Rotary cutter with wavy blade

Thread: khaki pearl cotton, red

1 (³⁄₈") button

Santa:

Pellon® Wonder-Under®

Fabric for appliqués: 1 red print
  scrap, 2 cream felt pieces

Purchased plain bib

Powdered blush and brush
  (optional)

Fine-tip permanent black fabric
  marker

Thread: cream pearl cotton, black

1 (³⁄₈") star-shaped button

Reindeer:

Pellon® Wonder-Under®

Fabric scraps for appliqués: red
  print, green print, tan print

Purchased plain bib

Powdered blush and brush
  (optional)

Fine-tip permanent black fabric
  marker

3 seed beads

Thread: khaki pearl cotton, black

1 (³⁄₈") button

Instructions

NOTE: If bibs will be washed frequently, outline motifs with coordinating dimensional fabric paint.

Buttons are used as accents in these projects, but French knots are recommended for children's clothing to prevent a possible hazard.

Mouse

1. Wash, dry, and iron bib and fabrics. Do not use fabric softener in washer or dryer.

2. Using patterns on page 101, trace 1 body, 1 sleeve, 1 hand, 1 package, 1 package tie, 1 scarf, 1 of each scarf tail, 1 hat, 1 hat tail, 1 of each ear, 1 hat fur, and 1 head onto paper side of Wonder-Under. Leaving approximate ½" margin, cut around Wonder-Under shapes. Press shapes onto wrong side of fabric scraps. Cut out shapes along pattern lines. Remove paper backing. Referring to photos, center and fuse shapes 1–13, in that order, to front of bib.

3. Using fabric marker, draw stitches around edges of ears, head, hat fur, hand, and entire scarf. Draw in eyes, nose, and whiskers. With rotary cutter, cut 1 (1" x 1½") rectangle from remaining red print. Cinch rectangle at middle and tie red thread in knot to secure. Hand-stitch bow onto appliquéd package.

4. Sew button at point of hat, using khaki thread. Tie knot on button front and cut ends short. In same manner, add fringe to scarf ends with 6 short khaki thread knots.

Santa

1. Wash, dry, and iron bib and fabrics. Do not use fabric softener in washer or dryer.

2. Using patterns on page 101, trace 1 beard, 1 hat, 1 hat fur, and 1 face onto paper side of Wonder-Under. Leaving approximate ½" margin, cut around Wonder-Under shapes. Press shapes onto wrong side of fabric scraps. Cut out shapes along pattern lines. Remove paper backing. Referring to photos, center and fuse shapes 1–4, in that order, to front of bib.

3. Using black thread, edgestitch along appliqué. Stitch star button to top of hat.

4. With black fabric marker, draw eyes on Santa face. If desired, add blush to Santa cheeks.

5. Wind several loops of pearl cotton thread into a 2"-long bundle. Secure loops in middle with knot. Stitch loops to front of beard for mustache.

Reindeer

1. Wash, dry, and iron bib and fabrics. Do not use fabric softener in washer or dryer.

2. Using patterns below, trace 1 face, 1 neck, 1 scarf, 1 of each scarf tie, 1 of each ear, and 2 holly leaves onto paper side of Wonder-Under. Leaving approximate ½" margin, cut around Wonder-Under shapes. Press shapes onto wrong side of fabric scraps. Cut out shapes

along pattern lines. Remove paper backing. Referring to photos, center and fuse shapes 1–7, in that order, to front of bib.

3. Using fabric marker, draw stitches around edges of appliqué, except for holly leaves. Draw in eyes and line for mouth. If desired, add blush to reindeer cheeks.

4. With red thread, stitch 3 beads to center of holly leaves. Sew button in place for nose, using black thread. Add fringe to scarf ends with 6 short khaki thread knots. Stitch antlers, using long stitches and khaki thread.

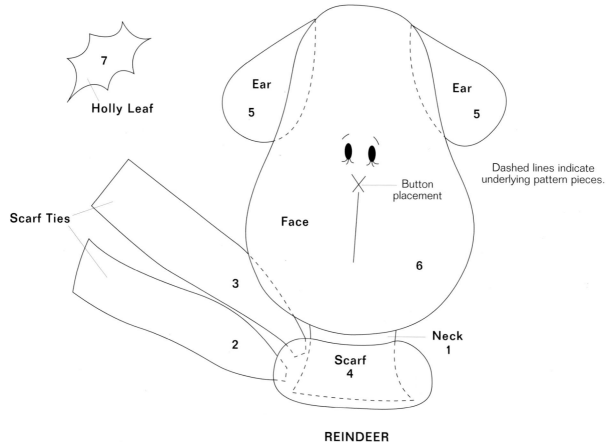

REINDEER

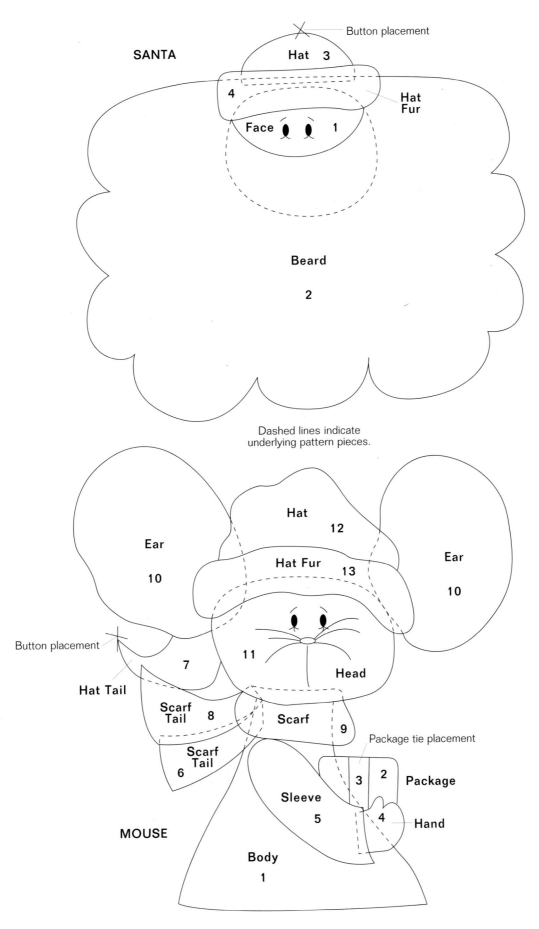

SANTA

Button placement

Hat 3

Hat Fur

4

Face 1

Beard

2

Dashed lines indicate underlying pattern pieces.

Ear

10

Hat

12

Hat Fur 13

Ear

10

Button placement

Hat Tail

7

11

Head

Scarf Tail 8

Scarf

9

Package tie placement

Scarf Tail

6

3 2 Package

Sleeve

5

4 Hand

MOUSE

Body

1

Candy Cane Slippers

Be festive right down to your toes in Christmas slippers that make up in a flash.

Materials

Pellon® Wonder-Under®
Red-and-white stripe fabric scrap
   for appliqués
1 pair purchased plain slippers
Red dimensional fabric paint in
   squeeze bottle
2 (½") white star-shaped buttons
White thread

Instructions

1. Using pattern, trace 2 candy canes and 2 reversed candy canes onto paper side of Wonder-Under. Leaving approximate ½" margin, cut around Wonder-Under shapes. Press shapes onto wrong side of fabric scraps. Cut out shapes along pattern lines. Remove paper backing. For each slipper, referring to photo, center and fuse candy canes on slipper toe.

2. Using dimensional fabric paint, outline candy cane appliqués. Let dry.

3. Stitch 1 button at center of each set of candy canes using white thread.

EXTRA: To make fusing easier, roll up a hand towel and stuff it into the slipper toe before applying the appliqué. The towel will keep the slipper supported until the appliqué is completely fused.

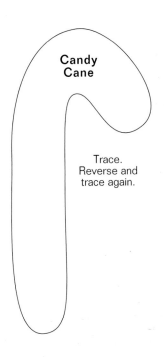

Candy Cane

Trace.
Reverse and
trace again.

Let It Snow

Snowflakes alight on soft or rugged fabrics with equal appeal.

Materials

Pellon® Wonder-Under®

⅛ yard silver organza

1 purchased plain gold T-shirt or
   long-sleeved denim shirt

Silver dimensional fabric paint in
   squeeze bottle

Instructions

1. For T-shirt, using pattern, trace 8 snowflakes onto paper side of Wonder-Under; **for denim shirt,** trace 7 snowflakes. **For each,** leaving approximate ½" margin, cut around Wonder-Under shapes. Press shapes onto wrong side of fabric. Cut out snowflakes along pattern lines. Referring to photo, center and fuse snowflakes onto shirt front.

2. For T-shirt, using fabric paint, outline snowflakes with solid paint line; **for denim shirt,** outline snowflakes with small evenly spaced dots. Let dry.

How different two purchased garments can turn out when using the same appliqué! The gold T-shirt (above) is a vivid contrast to the denim long-sleeved shirt (right).

Snowflake

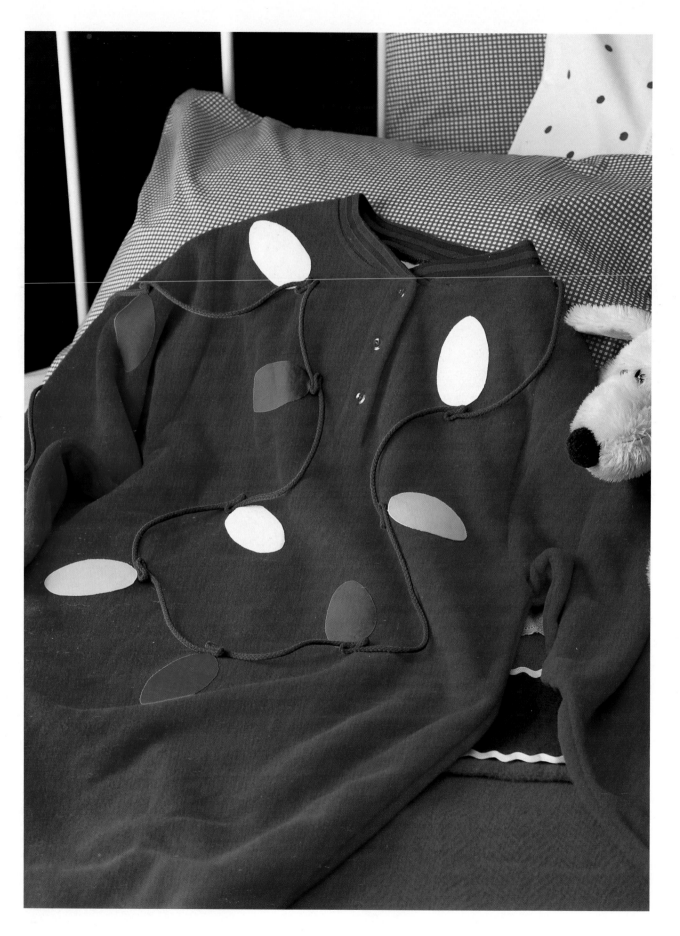

String-of-Lights Nightshirt

Brighten up bedtime apparel with colorful Christmas lights.

Materials

Purchased plain nightshirt
Assorted fabric scraps for
    appliqués: white, blue, green,
    yellow
Pellon® Wonder-Under®
Invisible thread
3 yards ¼" cotton cording

Instructions

NOTE: If nightshirt will be washed frequently, outline motifs with coordinating dimensional fabric paint.

1. Wash, dry, and iron nightshirt and fabrics. Do not use fabric softener in washer or dryer.

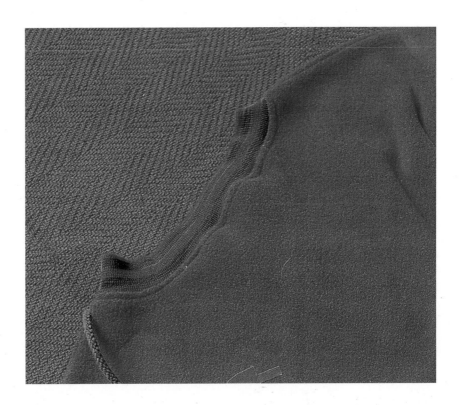

2. Using patterns, trace 12 lightbulbs and 1 base onto paper side of Wonder-Under. Leaving approximate ½" margin, cut around Wonder-Under shapes. Press shapes onto wrong side of fabric scraps. Cut out shapes along pattern lines. Remove paper backing. Set base aside. Referring to photo, randomly fuse lightbulb shapes to nightshirt front.

3. Using invisible thread, loosely wind and stitch cord around path of

lightbulbs, folding and stitching 2 (¾"-long) coils under each bulb (see photo at left). Carry 1 cord end over to back of nightshirt at 1 shoulder; stitch end in place. Fuse base on nightshirt back to cover cord end (see photo above).

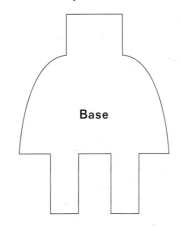

Base

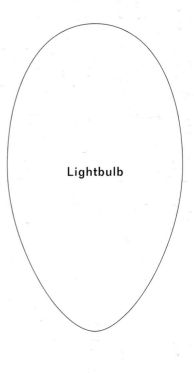

Lightbulb

Materials

½ yard red fabric
Pellon® Wonder-Under®
Lightweight cardboard
Craft knife
¼"-wide gold sticky-backed tape
Gold sequin snowflakes
Fabric glue
Rice paper

Instructions

1. Wash, dry, and iron fabric. Do not use fabric softener in washer or dryer.

2. Draw 1 (10" x 15") rectangle on paper side of Wonder-Under. Evenly divide rectangle into 3 (5" x 10") sections. Mark center fold line of each section lengthwise. Using patterns below and on page 112, trace 1 letter within each section to spell "Joy" on paper side of Wonder-Under. Press Wonder-Under onto 1 side of cardboard. Cut out areas along pattern lines. Lightly score cardboard along pattern fold lines on opposite side of cardboard, using

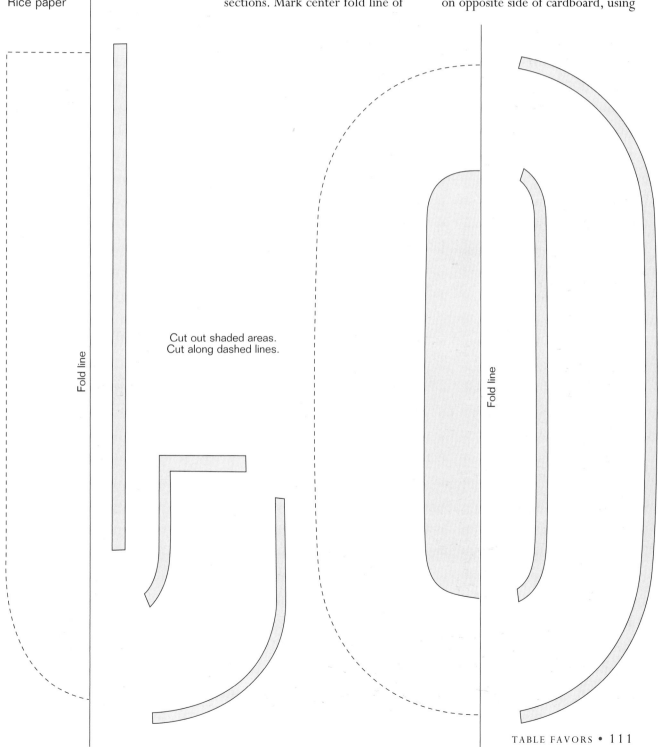

Fold line

Cut out shaded areas.
Cut along dashed lines.

Fold line

point of craft knife. Cut out rectangle. Remove paper backing. Fuse cardboard to wrong side of fabric. Cut fabric through cardboard letters and around panel. Trim fabric from edges.

3. Fold along scored lines and decorate edges with gold tape (see photo). Glue snowflakes randomly around panel with fabric glue.

4. Cut 1 (10" x 15") rectangle from rice paper. Glue rice paper to cardboard side of rectangle at corners and edges. Let dry. Fold rectangle along scored lines. After rectangle is standing, randomly glue paper to cardboard around letters (see photo). Let dry.

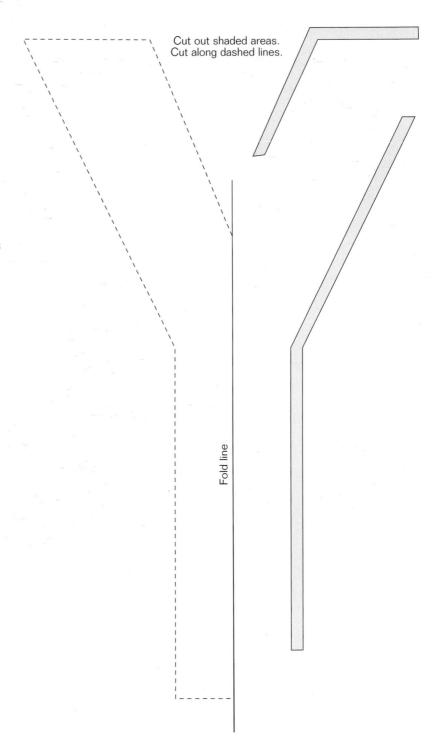

Cut out shaded areas.
Cut along dashed lines.

Fold line

Candle Collars

Scenic fabric, cardboard, and fusible web
team up to fashion these distinctive candle adornments.

Materials (Makes 1 collar.)

Measuring tape

Purchased plain candle

Small flute corrugated cardboard*

Large motif printed fabric**

Pellon® Wonder-Under®**

Hot-glue gun and glue sticks

* Corrugated cardboard is available
from Loose Ends. See page 144 for
more information.

** Yardage will depend on size of
desired candle and motif.

Instructions

NOTE: Do not leave burning candles
unattended.

1. Measure circumference and
height of candle. Using these measurements, cut 1 strip each from
cardboard and fabric, adding 1" to
each length.

2. Press Wonder-Under onto wrong
side of cut fabric piece. Remove
paper backing. Fuse fabric to cardboard. Trim top edge of candle
collar, following fabric design (see
photo).

3. Wrap collar around candle, leaving ¼" of space between cardboard
and candle. Overlap cardboard ends
and hot-glue in place.

Ornamental Tablecloth

Create a one-of-a-kind cover in a snap with bright holiday prints and ribbons.

Materials

Purchased 45"-square tablecloth

Fabric for appliqués: ⅛ yard each green print, blue print, and blue-and-red print

Pellon® Wonder-Under®

⅝ yard ⅛"-diameter gold cording

Straight pins

¾"-wide Pellon® Wonder-Under® fusible tape

Ribbons: ⅓ yard ½"-wide gold, 5½ yards ⅛"-wide green

Instructions

NOTE: If tablecloth will be washed frequently, outline motifs with coordinating dimensional fabric paint.

1. Wash, dry, and iron tablecloth and fabric. Do not use fabric softener in washer or dryer.

2. Using patterns, trace 4 of each ornament onto paper side of Wonder-Under. Press Wonder-Under onto wrong side of fabrics. Cut out shapes along pattern lines. Remove paper backing. Referring to photo, fuse ornaments around center of tablecloth. Press Wonder-Under onto wrong sides of remaining fabric scraps. Cut out decorative

shapes. Remove paper backing. Fuse shapes onto ornaments (see photo).

3. Cut 12 (2") lengths from gold cord. Pin each end of 1 cord at top of each ornament, forming loop.

4. Cut fusible tape into 1 (12") strip. Cut strip down to ½" wide. Press strip onto wrong side of gold ribbon. Remove paper backing. Cut ribbon into 12 (1") lengths. Referring to photo, fuse 1 length to top of each ornament, sandwiching looped cord in between. Remove pins.

5. To connect each ornament, measure distance between opposite pairs. Add 12" to each measurement; cut ribbon to measurement. Thread ribbon through looped cord on each pair; tie bow at each end.

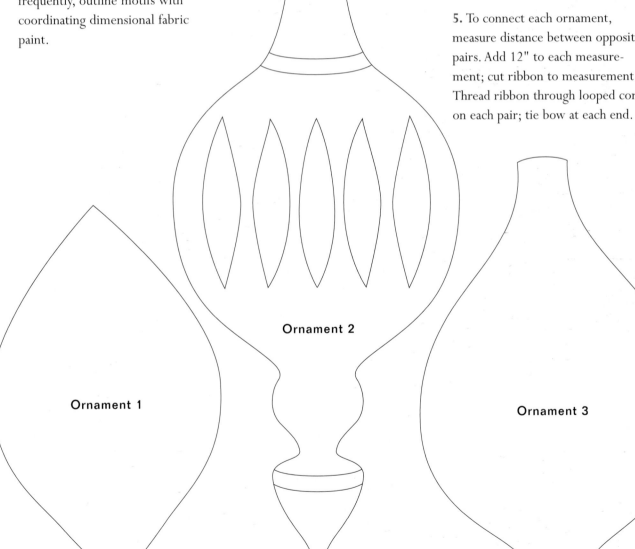

Ornament 2

Ornament 1

Ornament 3

Scrappy Coaster Set

Save your tabletops in style with a collage of
Christmas fabrics bound between layers of organza.

Materials (Makes 2 coasters.)

Pellon® Wonder-Under®
Fabrics: ¼ yard white organza,
  Christmas print fabric scraps
Thin craft batting
1 yard ⅜"-wide green satin ribbon
Pinking shears

Instructions

1. Press Wonder-Under onto wrong side of organza and batting. Cut batting into 2 (4") squares. Remove paper backing. Cut Christmas fabrics into desired shapes and sizes and layer pieces randomly on Wonder-Under side of batting squares. Keep edges clear of fabric.

2. **For each square,** cut ribbon into 4 (4") pieces. Position ribbon along edges of square (see photo). Fuse ribbon and fabric pieces to square.

3. Using pinking shears, cut 2 (5") squares from organza. Remove paper backing. Stack 1 organza square, Wonder-Under side up; 1 fabric scrap square faceup; and 1 organza square, Wonder-Under side down. Fuse squares together. Trim edges of organza with pinking shears if desired.

Cardinal Cachepot

Three-dimensional birds crafted from foam-core board and fabric
make this decoration soar with festive appeal.

Materials

Tracing paper

Pellon® Wonder-Under®

Fabric for appliqués: ⅛ yard each 2 green prints, ¼ yard each 3 red prints, ⅛ yard black

2 (4" x 8") green index cards

Fine-tip permanent black fabric marker

Foam-core board

Red thread

Hot-glue gun and glue sticks

Purchased plain cachepot

2 (¼") black buttons

Instructions

1. Using patterns, trace cardinal, wing, cardinal beak, and each holly leaf onto tracing paper. Cut around shapes.

2. Press Wonder-Under onto wrong side of each green print and 2 red print fabric pieces.

3. Cut index cards in half to make 4 (4") squares. Cut 2 (4") squares from each green fabric. Remove paper backing. Press 1 fabric square onto 1 side of each index-card square.

4. Using leaf patterns, trace and cut 4 leaves from fabric-covered index-card squares. Fold leaves at center and draw leaf veins with fabric marker.

5. Using cardinal and wing patterns, trace and cut 2 each of cardinal and wing from foam-core board. Cut 1 red print backed with Wonder-Under into 4 (8") squares and cut

remaining red print backed with Wonder-Under into 2 (4") squares. Remove paper backing. Fuse fabric to foam-core cardinals and wings. Trim around each piece to within ⅜" of edge. Fold and fuse fabric to foam-core edges.

6. Fuse remaining fabric pieces backed with Wonder-Under to other side of cardinals and wings. Trim fabric even with edges.

7. Using cardinal beak pattern, trace 2 cardinal beaks onto paper side of Wonder-Under. Leaving approximate ½" margin, cut around Wonder-Under shapes. Press shapes onto wrong side of black fabric. Cut out shapes along pattern lines. Remove paper backing. Referring to photo, fuse shapes to cardinals.

8. Using remaining red print, cut 6 (1⅛"-diameter) circles. Using red thread, handstitch small gathering stitches around edge of each circle. Pull thread to gather edge to center; tie off thread.

9. To assemble, hot-glue wings onto cardinals and cardinals onto center front of cachepot. Glue button eyes on cardinal faces. Referring to photo, glue holly leaves to cachepot beneath cardinals. Hot-glue gathered circles onto cardinals and cachepot for holly berries.

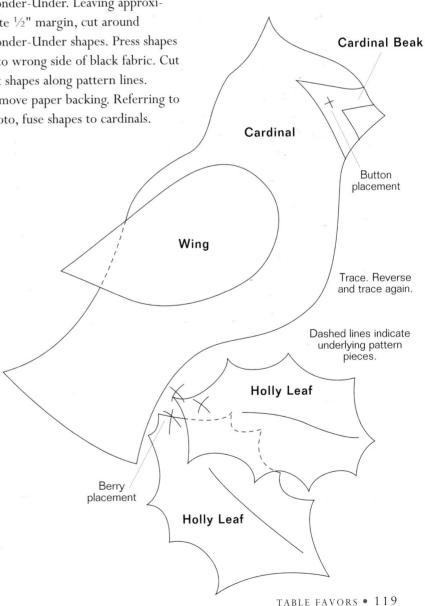

Cardinal Beak

Cardinal

Button placement

Wing

Trace. Reverse and trace again.

Dashed lines indicate underlying pattern pieces.

Holly Leaf

Berry placement

Holly Leaf

Chair Cover

Be a quick-change artist when you dress your chairs
in the colors of the season to complete your dinner table decor.

Materials (Makes 1 cover.)

Butcher paper

Chair

Straight pins

Fabrics: 72"-wide red felt*, 1½
   yards 45"-wide plaid flannel

Dressmaker's chalk

Pellon® Wonder-Under®

7 (⅝") buttons

* Yardage will depend on size of
chair.

Instructions

1. Using butcher paper, center and
trace seat pattern of desired chair.
Pin paper to center of felt. Then
measure seat back to floor, seat side
to floor, and seat front to floor.
Using chalk and referring to
Diagram, add measurements to seat
pattern, gradually increasing side
edges by total of 2". Cut out.

2. Press Wonder-Under onto wrong
side of flannel. Using ruler, draw
2½"-wide strips along bias of flannel on paper side of Wonder-Under.
Cut out strips along lines. Remove
paper backing. Referring to photo,
fuse flannel strips to cover felt
edges, leaving ½" at top for turning. Turn felt cover over and fuse
flannel edges down.

3. From remaining felt and flannel,
cut 1 (4" x 72") strip each. Remove
paper backing from flannel and fuse
to felt. Cut strip ends at point.
Measure and mark strip at center
and attach to chair at felt-cover center. Evenly space and stitch 3 buttons to strip center.

4. From flannel, cut 4 (1¼" x 12")
strips for felt cover ties. Remove

paper backing. Fold each tie in half
lengthwise and fuse. Cut 1 end of
each tie at point. Stitch each tie to
wrong side of cover, 5" from front
seat corners, along front and side
panels. Stitch 1 button to right side
of cover at each tie placement.

5. Place cover over chair. Tie cover
in place with corner ties.

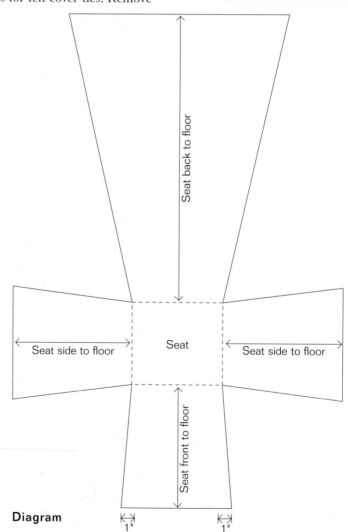

Diagram

Starry Table Runner

If you wish you may and wish you might have this table decoration tonight, you can complete this runner in a couple of hours.

Materials (Embellishes 88"-long table runner.)

Purchased plain table runner

¾"-wide Pellon® Wonder-Under® fusible tape

Ribbons: 3 yards each ⅜"-wide yellow, green, red, and blue grosgrain

Instructions

1. Wash, dry, and iron table runner. Do not use fabric softener in washer or dryer.

2. Cut fusible tape in half widthwise. Press tape onto ribbon.

3. For each large star, cut 10 (2½") lengths of ribbon. **For each medium star,** cut 10 (2") lengths of ribbon. **For each small star,** cut 10 (1¾") lengths of ribbon. **For each tiny star,** cut 10 (1½") lengths of ribbon.

4. From yellow ribbon, cut 1 tiny star, 2 small stars, and 3 medium stars. From green ribbon, cut 3 tiny

stars, 1 medium star, and 1 large star. From red ribbon, cut 2 small stars, 1 medium star, and 2 large stars. From blue ribbon, cut 2 tiny stars, 1 medium star, and 2 large stars. Remove paper backing from ribbon strips. Trim all ribbon ends straight.

5. Referring to photo, position ribbons in star shapes on right side of table runner. Overlap ribbon ends ¼" at star points. Fuse ribbon strips in place.

Tabletop Lanterns

Outfit a set of votive candle lanterns in fast fashion.

Materials (Makes 1 lantern.)

Pellon® Wonder-Under®

White organza

Heavyweight nonfusible interfacing

Votive candle

¾"-wide Pellon® Wonder-Under®
  fusible tape

Assorted ribbons and trims

Instructions

NOTE: Do not leave burning candles unattended.

1. Press Wonder-Under onto wrong side of organza. Remove paper backing. Fuse organza to interfacing. Cut interfacing to desired height and width of votive lantern, allowing for 1" overlap at ends.

2. Press fusible tape onto wrong side of ribbons and trims. Remove paper backing. Fuse ribbons and trims as desired to organza side of piece.

3. Press fusible tape to 1 short end of organza piece. Remove paper backing. Overlap opposite end and fuse ends together.

4. Carefully center lantern over lit votive candle.

Paneled Triptych

Your choice of fabrics makes this screen a unique tribute.

Materials

Craft paints: black, gold

Paintbrush

Purchased plain wooden trifold screen*

4 (25-mm) wooden beads

Pellon® Heavy Duty Wonder-Under®

Fabric scraps for appliqués

4 (1¼") wood screws

Screwdriver

* Trifold screen is available from Walnut Hollow. See page 144 for more information.

Instructions

1. Using black paint and paintbrush, paint front and back of paneled screen and each bead. Let dry. Paint beads with 1 coat of gold paint on top of black paint. Let dry.

2. Using patterns at right, trace 1 of each onto paper side of Wonder-Under. Leaving approximate ½" margin, cut around Wonder-Under shapes. Press shapes onto wrong side of fabric scraps. Cut out shapes along pattern lines. Remove paper backing. Referring to photo, fuse shapes to screen front. Cut pieces to fit around hinges.

3. Press Wonder-Under onto wrong side of remaining fabric scraps. Cut out squares and rectangles, ranging in sizes from ¼" x ⅝" to ½" x ¾". Remove paper backing. Fuse shapes to screen front.

4. Screw beads to screen bottom, using wood screws and screwdriver.

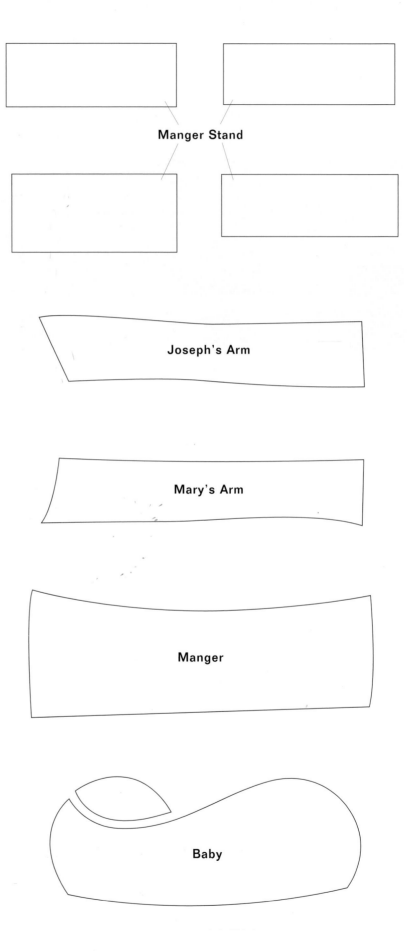

Manger Stand

Joseph's Arm

Mary's Arm

Manger

Baby

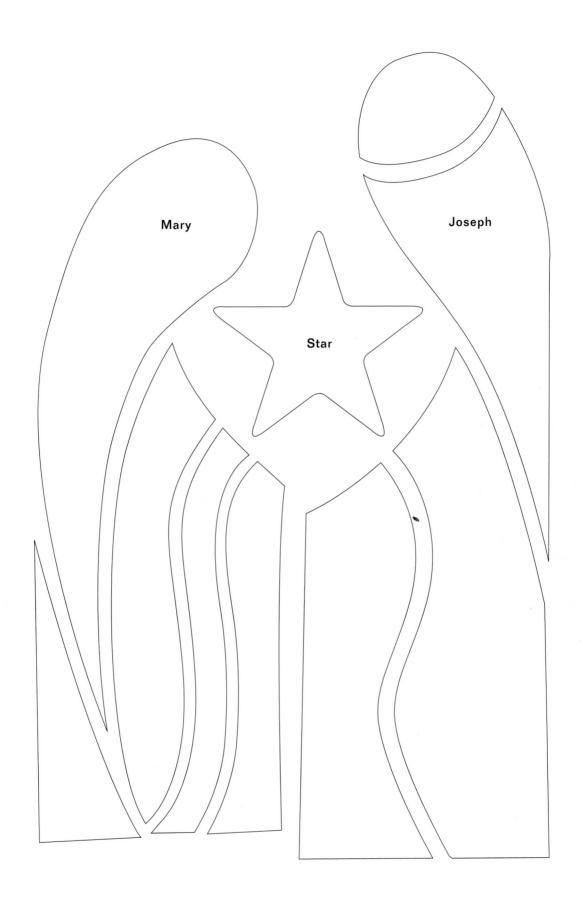

Mary

Joseph

Star

Penguin Place Mat and Napkins

These agile-on-ice creatures bring home the prize for pleasurable table decorations.

Materials (Makes 1 place mat and 1 napkin.)

Purchased place mat and napkin
Fabric scraps for appliqués
Pellon® Wonder-Under®
4 (4-mm) black beads
Thread: black, metallic silver

Instructions

NOTE: If place mat and napkin will be washed frequently, outline motifs with coordinating dimensional fabric paint.

1. Wash, dry, and iron place mat, napkin, and fabrics. Do not use fabric softener in washer or dryer.

2. Using patterns at right and on pages 130 and 131, trace 1 of each large penguin and 1 desired small penguin onto paper side of Wonder-Under. Press Wonder-Under onto wrong side of fabrics. Cut out shapes along pattern lines. Remove paper backing. Referring to photo, center and fuse large penguin shapes (in order marked) on right side of mat. Fuse small penguin shapes in order to 1 corner of napkin.

3. Using black thread, stitch 1 bead to each penguin for eye. Using long stitches and metallic thread, stitch curving line along each penguin foot for skates (see pattern).

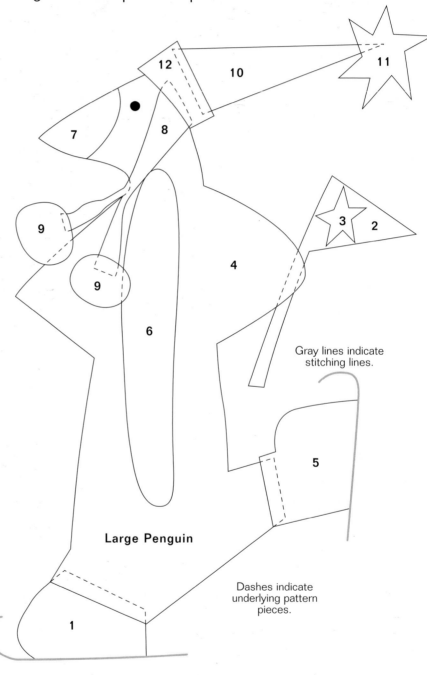

Gray lines indicate stitching lines.

Dashes indicate underlying pattern pieces.

Large Penguin

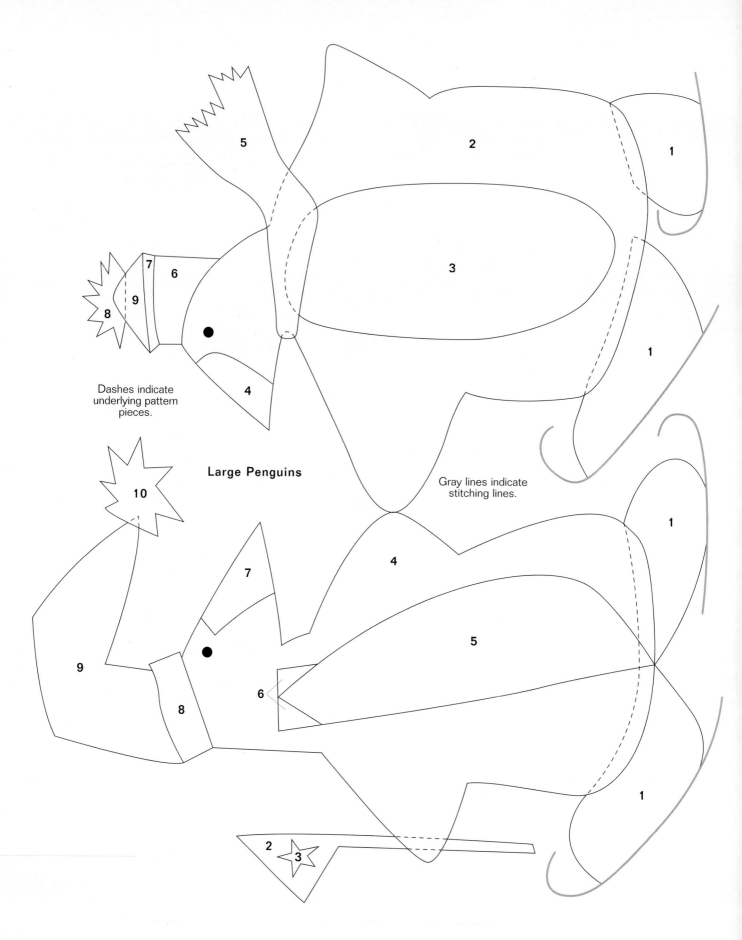

Large Penguins

Dashes indicate underlying pattern pieces.

Gray lines indicate stitching lines.

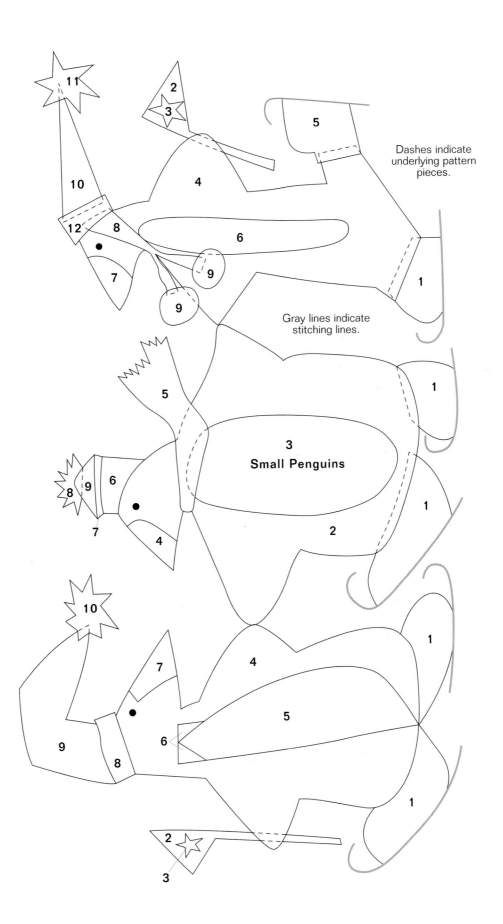

Dashes indicate underlying pattern pieces.

Gray lines indicate stitching lines.

Small Penguins

Tree Centerpiece

Star cutouts allow metallic fabric to gleam through
on this shining holiday decoration.

Materials

Pellon® Wonder-Under®
Green construction paper
Metallic gold fabric
Craft glue
¾" x 13" wooden dowel
5"-diameter round wooden plaque
Black craft paint
Paintbrush
1¼" wood screw
Screwdriver
Hot-glue gun and glue sticks

Instructions

1. Using patterns, trace 4 quarter-cone pattern pieces side by side to create 1 piece on paper side of Wonder-Under. Randomly trace small and large stars to cover cone. Press Wonder-Under onto 1 side of construction paper. Cut out stars and cone along pattern lines. Remove paper backing. Referring to photo, fuse gold fabric to paper. Trim paper even with cone edges. Using craft glue, overlap edges of cone and glue in place. Set aside.

2. Paint wooden dowel and plaque with black paint. Let dry. Using wood screw and screwdriver and working from bottom of plaque, attach dowel to plaque center.

3. Hot-glue cone to top of dowel.

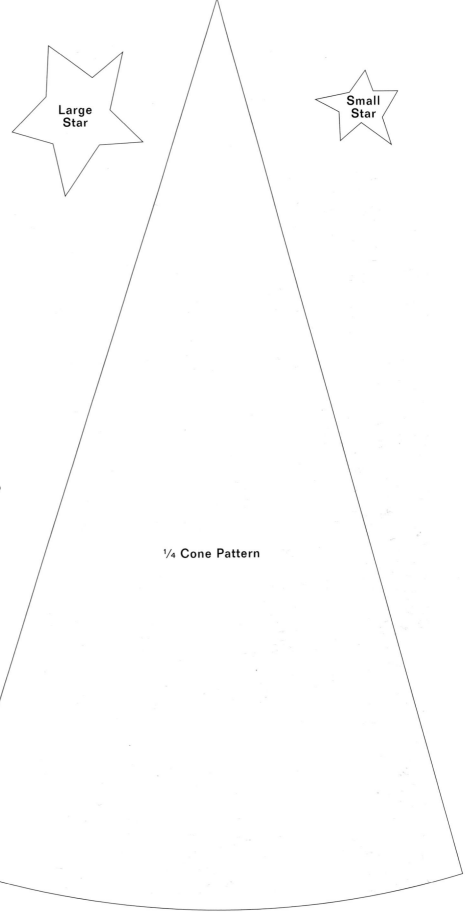

Large Star

Small Star

¼ **Cone Pattern**

Ribbons & Bows Bottle Cover

Spruce up a beverage bottle with a cover made from
velvet and oodles of shimmering ribbons.

Materials

Tracing paper

Green velvet

¾"-wide Pellon® Wonder-Under®
   fusible tape

Ribbons: 20" each assorted gold
   and white

Liquid ravel preventer

Green thread

1 yard ¼"-wide gold trim

Fabric glue

Instructions

1. Using patterns, trace and cut
2 triangles from tracing paper. Then
cut 2 triangles from green velvet.

2. Press fusible tape onto wrong
side of ribbons. Remove paper
backing. Evenly space ribbons diagonally across right side of 1 velvet
triangle (see photo). Trim each ribbon even with edges until triangle is
filled. Apply liquid ravel preventer
to cut ends.

3. With right sides facing and raw
edges aligned, stitch triangles
together, using ½" seam allowance.
Turn cover right side out. Turn bottom edge under ½" and edgestitch.

4. Cut gold trim into 5 equal
lengths. Tie each length in bow.
Randomly glue bows to front of
cover (see photo). Let dry.

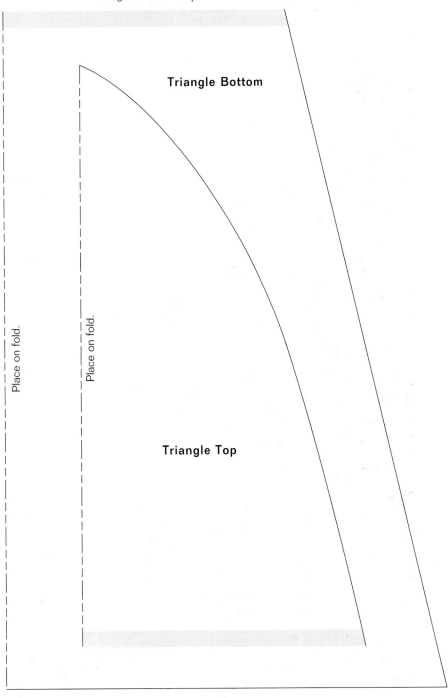

Overlap shaded areas of
triangle to continue pattern.

Triangle Bottom

Triangle Top

Place on fold.

Place on fold.

Holly for Your Table

Invite a traditional accent to dinner with this
jolly coordinating napkin ring and place mat.

Materials (Makes 1 place mat and 1 napkin ring.)

Fabrics: ¾ yard white, ½ yard green, red scraps
Pellon® Wonder-Under®
Coordinating thread
3 (⅜") buttons

Instructions

NOTE: If place mat and napkin ring will be washed frequently, outline motifs with coordinating dimensional fabric paint.

1. Wash, dry, and iron fabrics. Do not use fabric softener in washer or dryer.

2. Cut 1 (16"-diameter) circle from white fabric. Using patterns, trace 8 small leaves, 3 medium leaves, 9 large leaves, 1 napkin ring small leaf, 1 napkin ring large leaf, 10 small berries, and 15 large berries onto paper side of Wonder-Under. Press Wonder-Under onto wrong side of fabrics. Cut out shapes along pattern lines. Remove paper backing. Set aside napkin ring leaves and 3 small berries. Referring to photo, fuse leaves and berries around circle. Trim circle edges along outline of outer leaves.

3. Cut 1 (6" x 10") strip from Wonder-Under. Press Wonder-Under to wrong side of remaining white fabric. Cut out rectangle. Fold rectangle in thirds lengthwise, overlapping raw edges, and fuse. Trim ends.

4. Fuse remaining holly leaves and berries to center front of napkin ring (see photo).

5. Overlap short ends of rectangle to form ring. Stitch 3 buttons along center back of ring, stitching through all layers.

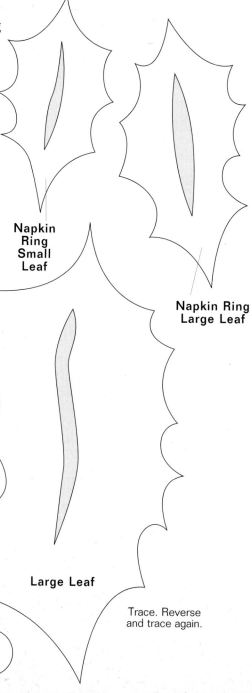

Napkin Ring Small Leaf

Napkin Ring Large Leaf

Cut out shaded areas.

Small Leaf

Trace. Reverse and trace again.

Trace. Reverse and trace again.

Large Leaf

Medium Leaf

Large Berry

Small Berry

Trace. Reverse and trace again.

Christmas Candy Keepers

These whimsical containers—a joyful jester's hat and merry mitten cartons—serve double duty as decorations and party favors.

Materials (Makes 1 candy holder.)

For each:

Pellon® Wonder-Under®

Hot-glue gun and glue sticks

Jester:

Compass

Fabrics: 6" x 18" silk, 6" x 12" metallic gold

3"-diameter cardboard circle

5 jingle bells

Metallic gold thread

Mittens:

Posterboard

Fabrics: 8"-square plaid flannel, 5"-square fleece

6" length 2"-wide grosgrain ribbon

8" length ¼" cotton cording

Instructions

Jester

1. Using pattern on page 141, trace 1 jester pattern onto paper side of Wonder-Under. Using compass, trace 1 (2¾"-diameter) circle onto paper side of Wonder-Under. Leaving approximately ½" margin, cut around Wonder-Under shapes. Press Wonder-Under onto wrong side of silk fabric. Cut out along pattern lines. Remove paper backing from both pieces, except from tab on jester pattern. Fuse jester piece to gold fabric. Trim gold fabric. Set circle aside.

2. Overlap ends of pattern to form ring with silk facing out. Remove paper backing from tab. Fuse tab in place.

3. Cut ½" notches along straight edge of jester ring. Insert cardboard circle at bottom of jester ring. Hot-glue notched edge of jester ring along cardboard edge. Fuse circle to bottom of jester bag.

4. Stitch bells to jester points with metallic thread.

Mittens

1. Using patterns on page 140, trace 4 mittens and 2 cuffs onto paper side of Wonder-Under. Leaving approximate ½" margin, cut around Wonder-Under shapes. Press 2 Wonder-Under mittens onto 1 side of posterboard. Cut out along pattern lines. Remove paper backing. Fuse mittens to wrong side of flannel and cuffs to wrong side of fleece. Press each remaining mitten to posterboard mittens. Remove paper backing and fuse to flannel. Trim flannel, following mitten pattern. Fuse 1 cuff to each mitten.

2. To make holder for candy, fold raw ribbon edges under ¼". Hot-glue edges in place. Hold ribbon in U shape along inside center of 1 mitten (see pattern). Apply hot-glue to mitten along U and set ribbon into glue. Hold ribbon in place until glue sets. Repeat for remaining mitten.

3. Fold cord in half and knot. Glue 1 end of cord to each inside corner of mitten bag (see photo).

Ribbon placement

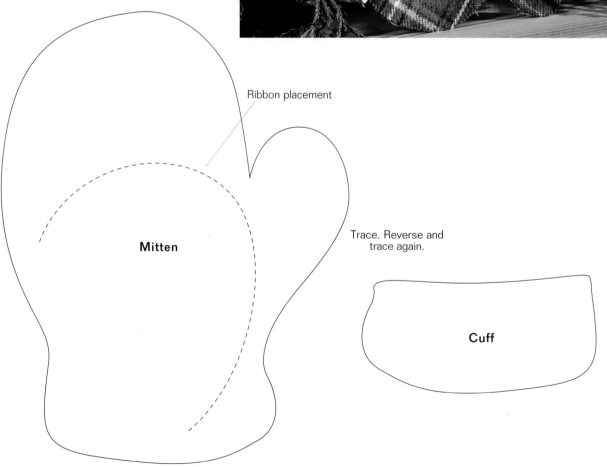

Mitten

Trace. Reverse and trace again.

Cuff

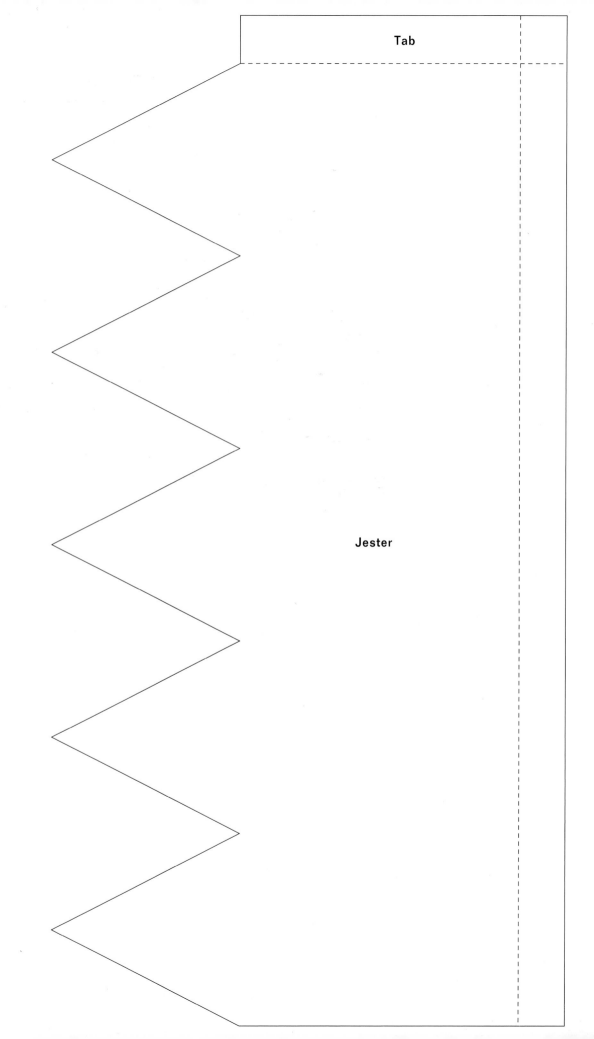

Tab

Jester

Merry Charger

Don't buy expensive Christmas china—make your own
patchwork creations to place under glass plates or to display as accents.

Materials

Craft paints: green, red
Paintbrush
Purchased plain wooden charger*
Clear varnish
Pellon® Heavy Duty Wonder-Under®
Fabric scraps for appliqués
Gold glitter dimensional paint in
   squeeze bottle

* Charger is available from Walnut
Hollow. See page 144 for more
information.

Instructions

1. Using green paint and paintbrush, paint front and back rim of
charger. Let dry. Apply 1 coat of
varnish over entire charger. Let dry.

2. Using patterns, trace 8 diamonds
and 17 triangles onto paper side of
Wonder-Under. Leaving approximate ½" margin, cut around
Wonder-Under shapes. Press shapes
onto wrong side of fabric scraps.
Cut out shapes along pattern lines.
Remove paper backing. Referring to
photo, fuse shapes to charger.

3. Using dimensional fabric paint,
draw gold swirls at center of plate
and between triangles and diamonds. Let dry. Paint 3 red dots
between triangles around charger
rim, using end of paintbrush.
Let dry.

4. Following manufacturer's instructions, apply final coat of varnish to
entire charger. Let dry.

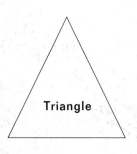

Triangle

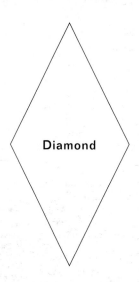

Diamond

Acknowledgments

Special thanks to the following people and companies for their valuable contributions toward project development:

Carol A. Burger

Kim Crane

Linda Hendrickson

Alisa Jane Hyde

Heidi Tyline King

Françoise Dudal Kirkman

Connie Matricardi

Dondra G. Parham

Catherine Pewitt

Betsy Cooper Scott

Sarah Stalie

Carol Tipton

Patricia Weaver

Lois Winston

We especially want to thank **Freudenberg Nonwovens,** in particular **Jane Schenck.**

Ordering Information

To locate a Pellon® Wonder-Under® retailer in your area, call 1-800-223-5275.

Contact Loose Ends at www.4loosends.com or call 1-503-390-7457.

Walnut Hollow products are available at leading craft departments throughout the country. For information on locating their products, call 1-800-950-5101.

144